TWINS AN

Audrey Sandbank, a chil
took several years' resear
to write this book. She is
and an older son, and li

TWINS
and the family

Audrey Sandbank

Illustrated by John Acton

ARROW BOOKS

Arrow Books Limited
62–65 Chandos Place, London WC2N 4NW

An imprint of Century Hutchinson Limited

London Melbourne Sydney Auckland
Johannesburg and agencies throughout
the world

First published in 1988

Printed and bound in Great Britain by
Anchor Brendon Limited, Tiptree, Essex

ISBN 0 09 956180 8

This book is dedicated to
my family

Contents

Acknowledgements

I would like to express my grateful thanks to all the parents, children and schools who gave their time in order to take part in the research into twins and family relationships which made this book possible.

I would also like to thank all my friends in the Twins and Multiple Births Association for their encouragement and enthusiasm, especially Dee Hoseason, Judi Linney, Jane Ellison and Judy Witts. I am indebted to Dr Elizabeth Bryan for her work on the biology of twinning and the loss of a twin, and to Jane Spillman for her work on maternal bonding.

Dr Burnham, Reader in Anthropology at University College, has been most helpful in checking through the anthropology and mythology section, but any errors in interpretation are entirely my own.

I would like to thank my colleagues, Gill Brown and Pat Freeman, for their helpful discussions and for reading through the manuscript.

I would also like to say how much I appreciated John Acton's delightful illustrations and the concept indexing by Jenny Rudge.

My fondest thanks go to my son Barry and daughters Amanda and Jennifer for providing the inspiration which led to my writing this book.

Finally I would like to thank my husband Charlie for his patient love and support during a rather long confinement, and for sharing those broken nights and night feeds after a rather shorter one all those years ago.

A. S.

Foreword

When the Twins and Multiple Births Association started in 1978 we were amazed to find how little written information was available for parents of twins, and indeed for the many professional groups concerned, who had tended to underestimate the various difficulties to which multiple births can give rise.

Since then the infant years have been well covered, but there is still a big gap in the literature on older twins. It is good to have this gap filled at last.

The special difficulties – as well, of course, as the joys – encountered by twins and their families are not limited to the early years. Problems concerning interdependence, individuality and competitiveness, for example, may continue throughout the lives of twins and can become worries for the twins themselves as well as for their parents and teachers.

As a family therapist, Audrey Sandbank has been helping twins and their families for many years. This experience, added to that of being a mother of twins herself, has most usefully qualified her to produce this invaluable and comprehensive book. It provides information, discussion and guidance for parents through all the stages of childhood and adolescence.

The friendly and accessible way in which Audrey Sandbank presents her advice will reassure many parents, not least with the discovery that they are not alone in facing the various problems that so often arise for families with multiple births.

Elizabeth Bryan MD MRCP DCH
Paediatrician
Consultant to the Twins and Multiple Births Association

Preface

My interest in twins began unexpectedly in December 1960, at the maternity hospital, when our eagerly awaited second baby turned out to be two little girls.

There were no twins clubs in those days and few books on twins. With only nineteen months between our older son and our two daughters, we were dropped in at the deep end and had to learn to swim. We made plenty of mistakes, but, like most parents of twins, we talked to other parents who had twins and compared notes.

During the last nine years I have been professionally involved in helping families find solutions to emotional and behavioural problems that they were experiencing with their children. Some of these children were twins, or the brothers and sisters of twins. Several of the parents were one of twins themselves. I became increasingly convinced that families with twins could experience difficulties that were specifically related to the twin situation.

Through my research into the effect of twins on family relationships and my association with the twins clubs, it was made clear to me that there was a general need for a book that offered information and practical guidance on bringing up twins of all ages and which included the older brother or sister. I must apologize to parents who have children that were born after their twins for featuring them so little in this book, but my brief has been chiefly to look at the difficulties that the older child may experience.

As is customary, I have used the male pronoun when talking in general terms, but no problem is the sole prerogative of any one sex. Parents may find the information they require featured under a different sex of twin from their own, or a different twin type. Parents may also find the answer to a question concerning one of their twins under the older brother or sister heading, and vice versa. The index is designed for quick reference.

The questions and answers that occur at the end of each section are to enable possible queries that may have occurred to readers to be dealt with in a straightforward manner and to give rather more specific advice on particular problems. Although I have been asked many such questions when speaking at meetings of parent groups, none has been included in its original form but all are generally typical of those which have featured regularly at such meetings.

My aim in writing this book has been to provide practical help whilst covering most aspects of twinning and being a twin that would be of interest to parents of twins and to twins themselves. Closely spaced brothers and sisters may sometimes experience similar problems to those of twins. The book could also be of help to those who are professionally involved in working with children, such as health visitors, teachers and therapists. Most people find the subject of twins fascinating and I hope that this book will be of general interest.

1

Twins in Anthropology and Mythology

1
The Roots of Twin Beliefs

If we are to understand the relationship between one twin and another and how he stands in relation to his family, we must go back to man's beginnings to take a deeper look inside ourselves.

In some societies, the belief about twins appears to have been that, along with breech births, deformed babies, and infants who cut their top teeth before their lower ones, they were uncanny, against nature, taboo. There was only one thing to be done – get rid of them as quickly as possible! However, twins were even more taboo than the luckless infant who cut its top teeth too soon, for they infected everything with which they came in contact: the mother, her belongings, and the hut in which they were born. All had to be destroyed. Because if, as they thought, two people could only make one baby, then who, or what, had fathered the second?

Early explorers, anthropologists and missionaries told similar stories. For example, Van Nyendael, writing in 1704, reported: 'They treat the twin-bearing woman very barbarously; for they actually kill both mother and infants and sacrifice them to a certain devil, which they fondly imagine harbours in a wood, near the village'; and Leonard, in 1906, told us, 'It is the standing law of the priests that no time is to be lost in removing the unfortunate twins. This is generally done by throwing them into the bush to be devoured by wild animals or, as is done by the Ibibio, Ibo and other coastal tribes, by setting them adrift on creeks in roughly made baskets of reeds and bulrushes when they are soon drowned or swallowed by sharks or crocodiles.' Nearer home, in the excavations at Court-St-Etienne in Belgium, pairs of small funeral urns were found enclosed in a larger adult one dating back to 500 BC.

Many a good wife must have been killed and perhaps those who were rather fond of their wives questioned the necessity of her following her children. We do not know, but we find that in other areas purification rites took place and the wife was more to be pitied than blamed, but she might still be banished to live with other mothers who had given birth to twins so that a curse did not fall on the whole tribe. However, even if it was decided that the mother was more of an innocent victim than a willing adulteress, the problem still remained – who was responsible for the second baby?

Various peoples came up with different possibilities. Perhaps it was the ghost of an ancestor, perhaps a spirit from the woods, but far and away the most popular theory was that the baby had come down from the sky, from the thunder and lightning which sent the wind and the rain, and perhaps birds, particularly the birds with red on their feathers like the woodpecker.

If only one twin has a spirit parent, then it can be argued that only one twin needs to die, the other being the normal mortal offspring of its natural parents. Where this practice was followed it was often believed that both the parents, but particularly the father and the surviving twin, were still in a great deal of danger from the evil wishing of the thunder child. Travellers in East Africa reported more than one instance of the father killing one of the children by putting a lump of earth in its mouth (perhaps to anchor the spirit). If this was not done it was said that the father would lose his virility. The Chagga in East Africa believed that if the baby was allowed to live it would grow up to kill both its parents. To protect the living child a representation of the twin was made as an earthly home for its spirit to live in so that it would not be lonely and come to fetch its brother or sister. Regular sacrifices of food were made to the image so that it did not become jealous or feel neglected.

The decision as to which child had the spirit parent was usually decided by expediency. If the twins were a boy/girl pair, then it was the girl that had to be killed because boys were considered to be more useful. If they were same-sex twins then it was usually the first born or sometimes the strongest baby. The Ibo called the first born 'In'meabo' which means 'two children'. At Brass, where the first born was kept, if the child was male it was called 'Isele' and if female 'Sela'. Both names mean 'selected'. In Zululand a twin who was saved had no name until he was sixteen, and one particular chief's son acquired the name 'Hatred', which obviously summed up the way his parents felt about his being a twin!

From Burma, Cambodia and the Malay Archipelago and the areas of Polynesia, Melanesia and Western Australia, there were reports of the particular dislike of mixed-sex twins who were frequently both killed because of the concern that, whilst still in the womb, they had broken the local laws concerning marriage. There was one that told of mixed-sex twins being called betrothed twins and that in former times they had married one another when they had reached maturity.

Not all peoples were in agreement about which child was the elder. Some believed that the first child had been sent on ahead to announce the arrival of the elder child. The Igala of the Upper Niger believed that the elder child had remained behind as a token of his superiority. Tribes in the Yoruba country called the firstborn 'Taiwo' which means that he came to inspect the world for the senior twin called 'Kehinde'. In Japan today the second-born twin is believed to be the elder. It has been described as being similar to two people getting out of a bus: the first one getting on is the last one to get off!

Dr Philip Burnham told me of his experiences amongst the Gbaya of Cameroon and the Central African Republic who believe that every man is accompanied by his spirit body called 'so-te'. When twins are born it is thought that the spirit body has manifested itself as the double of the child, a sort of doppelganger.

When both twins were allowed to live, mother and twins were sometimes exiled to twin towns and twin islands. Some of their belongings were considered unclean, various payments were made to the chief or medicine man, or an expensive celebration given which had its roots in purification rites.

There are still beliefs that the twins and their mother might taint the cattle, the crops or the tribal fortunes. However, others believe instead that they have more positive magical powers. Their help may be enlisted in fertility rites, they are thought to be able to influence the weather, to have special healing powers and foretell the future. In Sierre Leone twins used to be employed to administer medicine and they set up temporary twin temples which appeared to represent the basis of a twin priesthood.

The Baronga of South Africa called twins 'Bana-ba-Tilo', meaning 'Children of the Sky', and they shared the role of rainmaker with their mother. The Nuer called a twin 'Ram Nhial',

a 'Person of the Sky'. In some areas, apart from their relationship to the thunder, lightning and sky, they were also said to have a special relationship to certain creatures: the monkey, bear, wolf, even salmon, and the thunder bird, a bird with red on its feathers. Where this special relationship existed there were taboos. The twins were not allowed to eat the flesh of these totem creatures or even eat from a pot in which they had been cooked. The Nilotic Nuer of Uganda believed that twins were birds and a twin would say to a bird, 'Oh bird, I am a twin, you are a twin.' Twin babies who died were said to have 'flown away', a nice thought. Amongst the Nuer there was not only a taboo on eating the flesh of birds, but also eggs. A report in 1936 tells of a girl who would not eat fish, crocodile or turtle, because they laid eggs. Adult men would avoid eating birds unless they were actually in a state of famine, although the children, if they were not twins, were allowed to catch and eat them. Twins throughout the world used to be enlisted to bring good fortune to hunting or fishing expeditions, particularly when hunting the twins' totem creature.

Even in Great Britain at the beginning of this century, there could be found traces of twin beliefs. They were invited as special guests to weddings, rather like the lucky sweep, and a Welshman whose cow gave birth to twins quickly sold it.

Later writings by William Bascom on the Yoruba showed that in the late 1930s there was still a wealth of material on twins. The tradition of making small carved figures called 'ere-Ibeji' to symbolise the twins and to be kept by the surviving twin – or the parents when both died – continues to this day. There is a high twinning rate amongst the Yoruba, particularly in the rural areas, which may be due to eating a certain species of yam.

We have looked at some of the beliefs about twins, but what about their management?

Equal treatment of twins is something about which many peoples appeared to agree. On the Upper Congo at the beginning of the century, the mother not only had to reserve one breast for each child, but the food she ate herself had to be cooked and eaten in two separate pots and she ate from right and left pots with right and left hands. If she did not do this it was said that one of the twins would die. In Togoland the mother had to divide her food into equal portions and eat simultaneously from each so that both twins should be equally nourished. Again, if she failed to do this, the neglected child was supposed to get cross and die. In Angola the Bihe scrupulously divided the twins' food into two portions, and when they were given a present, identical presents had to be held out to them, one in each hand. In the Congo region the twin born first was always carried on the right arm and the second on the left, and again they had to have identical presents 'or there is grief to one'. A familiar problem!

Twins were expected to cry together and rejoice together. A sad little story tells of how one young girl was given more than forty stripes because that was what her guilty twin sister had received. No problem in that tribe in deciding which twin was to blame when neither would own up. Not much point in one twin owning up come to that!

The problems of looking after twins single-handed used to have more practical solutions than those often provided today by modern communities. Amongst the Buganda 'paternity leave' was granted until after the next war expedition, whilst the Shuswap Indian had to take his turn with his wife in staying at home to look after the twins as it was difficult to carry them around in the traditional way. They also had to wash the twins with fir branches every day. The

Masai of East Africa assigned another woman of the Kraal to assist in bringing up the twins on a long-term basis.

Equal treatment in some cases extended to marriage. In Angola both twin girls had to marry the same husband and there was a case of twin brothers both having to marry the same girl. Others felt that the special relationship between the twins had to be acknowledged. In Bali there was a time when mixed-sex twins were married to each other, but among the Nilotic Nuer same-sex twins only had to go through a form of mock marriage to each other before they were free either to have sexual relations or contract a real marriage to someone else. All the guests at the mock marriage had to dress up in the clothes of the opposite sex. The natives of Savu, a small island between Java and New Guinea, thought that mixed-sex twins drained each others' strength and they dreaded the possibility of a marriage between them. This was why one, usually the girl, was killed at birth.

Amongst the Buganda and the Yoruba, equal treatment extended beyond the grave. They dressed the image of the dead twin in the likeness of the survivor, even giving it the same necklaces and bracelets and offering it the same food. These images can still be found in Nigeria today. The Buganda went further: even the twins' graves had to be identical.

There seems to have been a strong belief that twins had the power to cause death. The Yoruba believed that twins could kill the parent of the same sex as themselves when they grew up, whilst the Nilotic Nuer thought that they would kill the parent of the opposite sex. However, if they were of mixed sexes they would each champion one parent, so the parents would live. On the Upper Congo there was a belief that if one twin died it was because the other twin wanted to be on his own and had wished his death.

Beliefs about the possibility of telepathy between twins can also be traced. The reason given for killing one of a pair of twins by the Atonga was that each twin felt the other's pain even at a distance, so that if they both lived they would experience double the pain in their lives!

One final note on the treatment of twins. In Angola when twins were dying, no medical aid was given. 'Our god,' they said 'has done this deed of creating terrible twins, and he must kill or cure them.'

2
Myths and Legends

Many of the myths and legends that have been told throughout the world seem to have strong links with twin practices and beliefs.

An important ingredient in many of these stories concerns twins quarrelling in the womb. This is not very surprising when there have been conflicting views on which twin was the elder, the first-born or the second-born. Not only the rights of inheritance, but perhaps life itself, depended on the outcome.

Another basic ingredient is the opposing characters of the twins which may contain one or more of the following contrasting elements: one is good, the other evil; one is smooth, the other hairy; one is fair, the other dark; one the artist, the other the man of action; one mild tempered, the other fiery; one stays at home, the other ventures out into the world; one is a builder, the other a hunter. There are further, often shared, attributes which exist side by side with those already mentioned – those of agriculturist, horserider, healer, winner of battles. Most stories include an attempt to steal the birthright, or a fight between the twins, and occasionally both. In some it is the weaker twin who wins by trickery, but often it is the stronger twin, particularly if he has been fathered by one of the gods. Non-identical twins would have had a better chance of survival than identical twins and this may be why these legendary twins are so often physically different. The 'Couple Effect' (see chapter eight) would accentuate differences in character, whatever the twin type.

The story of Romulus and Remus appears to follow very closely the early twin practices. Their mother was killed and they were cast afloat on the waters of the Tiber, eventually to be brought up by a wolf. They were builders (mythology credits them with the building of Rome; twins are traditionally credited with teaching people new trades, particularly building and boat-building) and finally Romulus kills Remus and disappears in a clap of thunder.

A similar story to that of Romulus and Remus is the Theban story of Zethos and Amphion. They were the twin sons of Antiope; their supernatural father was Zeus and natural father Epopeus, who died of shame at his wife's adultery. Epopeus left it to his brother to punish his wife and kill the twins. The children were left to die on the top of a mountain, just as they would have been in West Africa at the beginning of this century. They are rescued by a shepherd who finds out the secret of their birth. They finally save their mother from being killed by a spirit and Amphion is said to have helped build Thebes, which, it has been suggested, was originally a twin town. The story of Oedipus may have developed from an earlier twin myth. He was left to die as a baby because if he grew up he would kill his father, a common belief concerning twin boys, and he was given the kingdom of Thebes – again the twin town.

Legends of prenatal struggles between twins include the ancient Persian myth concerning twins Ormuzd and Ahriman. Ahriman was the evil one, the spirit child, and should have been the younger. He overheard his father saying that the first-born would inherit the kingdom, so he struggled to change places with his sweet-natured brother in the womb and succeeded in keeping the inheritance from his brother for nine thousand years. Justkeha and Tarviskara were similar North American Indian mythological twins who quarrelled in the womb and continued to be opposing principles of good and evil in the world. There is a biblical story along the same lines that tells of Pharez pushing his brother Zarah aside as they were in the process of being born, and a Greek one about brothers Proitus and Akrisios. They quarrelled in the womb and the younger brother also finally triumphed over his elder twin.

Perhaps the most well known of all stories is that of Esau and Jacob. Jacob, the gentle shepherd, cheats his hunter brother of his birthright, but they later make their peace with one another. An early explorer, Captain Merker, reported that the Masai of East Africa had a very similar story, and there may well be some link as the Masai also had an Exodus story, and one concerning the Giving of the Law – only Mount Kilimanjaro was substituted for Mount Sinai.

Other stories deal with the danger to the mortal twin of his immortal brother. The Ao-Nagas of Assam tell of twin heroes who were always quarrelling. The elder twin turns the younger into a squirrel and, like Romulus, goes off to live in the sky where he deploys the odd flash of lightening as a reminder that 'big brother is watching you'! The Scandinavian god Hoder killed his brother Balder when they quarrelled over a goddess, and there is an ancient Phoenician story of quarrelling twins Hypsouranios and Usous, one a builder, the other a hunter. The story tells of one particularly violent quarrel accompanied by a tremendous thunder-storm. However, instead of one brother disappearing into the sky, the forest catches fire and Usous takes advantage of the situation by breaking the branches off a burnt-out tree and turning it into a boat. He becomes the first boatbuilder. The twins are learning to cope with their differences!

So we reach the next group of myths. Both twins are seen as good, although one may still be mortal and the other immortal. The Greek Castor takes the decision to share his immortality with Pollux when his twin is dying, and they spend alternate periods in heaven and on earth by kind permission of Zeus, the thunder god. Castor and Pollux become the Dioscuri, children of Zeus.

These heavenly twins became associated with the morning star and evening star which were thought to be two separate spheres. The stars called Gemini (twins) have sometimes been commonly called by the Greeks, Castor and Pollux, but have also been called Jason (Jasion) and Tryptolemos, and sometimes Apollo and Heracles (the female twin Artemis has been replaced by a male twin).

Amongst primitive peoples there was a deep-seated fear of loss when the sun went down. Many myths and fairytales owe their origin to the heroic rescuing of the sun by heavenly twins, one brother going east and the other west. Jason and the Argonauts went in search of the 'Golden Fleece'. Many of his crew were one of twins as was Jason himself. Other stories tell of the rescue of a woman who, it appears, represents the sun. For example, the Acvins, twin chariot drivers, rescued Sury, the daughter of the sun, and came to be regarded as saviours of people in distress who could open the eyes of the blind. The Persian religion also had its Acpino Yarvino, the Acpins, and clearly they are related.

Twins are also involved in creation legends, perhaps because of their connection with fertility. The Crow, Kiowa and Shoshonean Indian tribes have stories of twin gods created by being cut in half by divine intervention when they were boys. The Incas of Peru had a creation legend concerning twin brothers Apocatequil and Piguerao, who emerged from two eggs. Apocatequil appears to have been the immortal brother. The ten tribes of Israel were said to be descended from Jacob's ten sons who each married their twin sister.

Divine twins, particularly the Dioscuri, were believed to be able to help in battle. In a Theban legend the Locrians prayed to the Dioscuri for success in the Battle of the Sagras River and miraculously two horsemen appeared of strange appearance and unusual size, wearing red cloaks and riding white horses, who quickly turned the tide of battle. In Britain a story is told of twin ploughmen who saved the day for the Scots against the invading Danes.

With the spread of Christianity these twin gods became saints. In the Byzantine and other calendars we find Florus and Laurus, or Frol and Lavior as they were known in Russia. It is interesting that when the Peruvians became Christians under the influence of the Spaniards, they changed the name of one of twins from the Peruvian 'son of lightning' to the name 'Santiago'. They had learned from their Spanish teachers that St James (Santiago, San Diego) and St John had been called 'Boanerges' – sons of thunder – by Jesus. However, it was the apostle Thomas who was most likely to have been a twin as his name comes from the Hebrew word for twin and he was also known as Didymus, the Greek name for twin. There is no doubt that being a twin has had a deep religious significance in many cultures.

2
Under Fives

3
Family Relationships

Parents

With modern ultrasound scanning most mothers nowadays are told that they are expecting twins quite early in their pregnancy, but many parents who are reading this book may have older twins and it used not to be at all unusual to hear the news for the first time in the delivery room.

Whenever the news is received, there can be mixed feelings: there may be worries about an extra mouth to feed, the effect on an older child, or very natural fears about looking after two babies. Whatever twins are, they are not planned!

But it is not all gloom and doom. Many parents are delighted by the idea of having twins for nature has provided them with the unexpected, a fresh challenge, an extra bonus. They may be the fulfilment of a secret wish. There is the excitement of anticipation, suddenly noticing other people's twins and wondering what one's own will be like. For those who may not want to go through another pregnancy, particularly older parents for whom twins sometimes arrive as a late gift, there is the knowledge that twins provide each other with a ready-made playmate. Finally, parents of twins automatically become eligible for membership of the Twins and Multiple Births Association, run by its members, with many local branches that give help and support.

After the birth, twins are more likely to need extra medical attention and their average birth weight is lower than singles, which may mean a longer stay in hospital for one or both twins. Should the mother wish to breast-feed there can be several obstacles in the way: the supply may be insufficient for more than one baby (though it can be topped up with a bottle), the twins may be too small to suckle, or there may be a problem of physical distance if the mother is allowed to return home before the twins or with only one. A determined mother can sometimes overcome these obstacles, but there may be a delay before twins can both be breast-fed. Twins are therefore much more likely to be bottle-fed.

No mother automatically adores the little bundle put in her arms, let alone two. We all take our own time to get to know our babies. This time may be lengthened in the case of twins because of post-natal tiredness, after a rather more demanding pregnancy, and lack of opportunity. It can also be confusing to be presented with two babies, particularly if they are identical.

It seems that one way mothers may get round this problem is to get to know them one at a time. This is usually a quite unconscious choice, but it has been noticed that new mothers often pick up the heaviest baby first and find him easier to look after. There may be other reasons why one twin is the favourite. It may be the first baby to arrive home. One baby may seem prettier than the other or look like someone in the family that the mother is close to. It may be the smallest baby that makes the mother feel protective.

The less-preferred baby sometimes has a higher-pitched, more aggravating cry. Some premature single babies also cry like this and it can cause anxiety in the mother. However, surprisingly, the less-preferred baby has also been reported as being the better sleeper. Usually if there is a preference it doesn't last very long, long enough, perhaps, for the mother to get over the birth and feel that there is enough of her to go round two, but it is not at all unusual for the preference to persist.

It seems that another way of learning to love two babies, who may look so alike that it is difficult to tell them apart, is to be much more aware of differences in their personalities. Each baby is seen as a very separate person requiring equal but different responses. It has been found that parents of identical twins see them as almost as different from each other as non-identical twins in the first two years of life, which may be partly due to the time lag in growth and the learning of new skills. As they grow older parents tend to see them as more alike.

There is sometimes a tendency with mixed-sex twins to treat the less physically mature male twin as the baby of the family. Although this will encourage the female twin to be independent and protective towards her brother, she may be losing out on some of the cuddles and he may become a little less adventurous.

In the early days mothers may feel tired and depressed and

inclined to skip meals. It is better to skip the housework than the two essentials of food and rest. Getting out of the house is important too, particularly both parents together, even if it is only for an hour or so for a drink, a quiet drive or a walk if the weather is fine. Parents need their own space and time to be together and adjust to their new situation.

There is also another side to becoming the mother of twins, which I will discuss again later: that of changing her view of herself. It may be that she sometimes sees herself as marooned with her children, overwhelmed by the odds, but there are few mothers who do not have a certain pride in their unexpected achievement and an increased sense of confidence.

Most mothers receive some help after the birth from either husband, relatives or friends. Parents of twins are much more likely to welcome the help of grandparents where, if there had only been one baby, they might have been inclined to go it alone. A sea-change often comes over an expectant mother once she knows she is expecting two or more, and grandparents can be delighted to find that they are needed, not only after the birth, but in the months to come.

The father's involvement with looking after the new babies varies enormously. The most unlikely husbands may find themselves knee-deep in nappies, taking their turn bottle-feeding the twins, and, much to their surprise, actually enjoying it. Other fathers, who perhaps would like to be involved, may lack the confidence to offer help when faced with two small babies or a mother who appears to be so preoccupied with the twins that there seems to be no room for him. No father should underrate his importance to his family and the father of twins can be invaluable in helping the mother to avoid a feeling of isolation. Parents working together can often think of practical answers to day-to-day problems and can offer a useful model to twins.

What is the difference between an identical and a non-identical twin?

Identical twins are also known as uniovular or monozygotic (MZ) twins. This is because they come from one ovum, or egg, which is fertilized by one sperm which then becomes a zygote, or germ cell.

NAPPIES

This zygote then splits into two cells which eventually grow into two genetically identical babies. If the two cells remain partly attached they may grow into conjoined ('siamese') twins.

Non-identical twins, sometimes called fraternal twins, are also known as binovular or dizygotic (DZ) twins. This is because they come from two separate eggs, fertilized by two separate sperms which each becomes a zygote with a different set of instructions, or genes. Fertilization can take place at different times within the same menstrual cycle. They eventually grow into two very different babies who are no more alike than ordinary brothers or sisters. Mixed-sex, or unlike-sexed, twins can never be identical.

How likely am I to conceive twins?

There may be many more twins conceived than are actually born. This is because in the first few weeks one twin's gestational sac sometimes just disappears. It appears on the first ultrasound scan, but by the time the next one is taken there is no trace of it. For this reason mothers are not usually told that they are expecting twins until after fourteen weeks of pregnancy, when there is a good likelihood that both fetuses will continue to grow normally. You have a one per cent chance of being delivered of twins, but this chance is increased if you have been taking drugs to induce ovulation, in other words a fertility drug.

I married late and would like to have a baby. I've been told that because of my age I might have fraternal twins. Is this true?

It has been found that the average age of mothers of non-identical twins is higher than that of mothers of single children or identical twins. However, this is no guarantee, I'm afraid, that you will have twins.

Other factors that have been found to influence the chance of a woman having twins are:

Being taller than average
Being heavier than average
Having regular closely spaced periods
Onset of periods earlier than average

A family history of twins
Having a large family already
Conceiving very easily

Unfortunately twins sometimes arrive before you've had the chance to find out if you conceive easily!

We are expecting twins. What is the chance that they will be identical and how will we know if they are?

To answer the first part of your question. One third of all twins born in Western Europe are identical, so the chance that you will have identical twins is one in three. The other two-thirds are fraternal, non-identical, twins. However, the fraternal twinning rate is not the same throughout the world and if you came from Japan or China, for example, where the fraternal twinning rate is low, it would be much more likely that you would be expecting identical twins. In China, more than one child per family is officially frowned on, and the birth of a second child may incur financial penalties as well as the disapproval of the community. However, the birth of twins is the exception, and parents of twins consider themselves to be particularly fortunate. Nigeria has the highest incidence of fraternal twins and if you came from Nigeria there would be a higher probability that you were expecting non-identical twins. However it has been suggested that part of the reason for the high fraternal twinning rate in Nigeria has been due to eating a certain species of yam, so that when the diet is changed the fraternal twinning rate would be reduced. In other words if you come from Nigeria, but are living in England, you would only have a slightly higher chance of having fraternal twins. If you are of Asian Indian origin you would have a slightly lower chance, but not as low as someone from Japan. The incidence of identical twins, one in every three hundred births, is similar throughout the world.

Now, how would you be able to be sure if your twins were identical? If the outermost placental membrane enveloping the fetus, the chorion, is shared by both twins, then the doctor can safely say that the twins are identical. It used to be thought that if this was not the case the twins were non-identical, but it has since been discovered that about a third of identical twins have separate chorions. In these cases, how can we tell the identical twin from the non-identical twin? Principally by blood which can be taken from twins at any age, but can also be taken from the umbilical cords of the placenta after birth. The tests will determine the blood groups and also biochemical markers, e.g. enzymes and protein types. However these tests are not done as a matter of routine after every twin birth. If only one test shows a difference, then the twins are not identical.

If twins are not blood tested at birth and parents wish to be sure about the zygosity, twin type, of their twins, then the GP can occasionally arrange routine blood tests at the local hospital. These will not give quite as accurate a picture as those done by special genetics laboratories which do a very wide range of tests. Where older twins are concerned, the parents' own judgement has been found to be a very good guide to the zygosity of their twins. Fingerprinting, though easy, is not a reliable method of determining twin type.

I've been taking a drug to induce ovulation. What is the risk of my having triplets?

About one in every two hundred of those taking a fertility drug have triplets. The risk of having twins is much higher: one study showed that it could be as high as eleven in every hundred.

We've been told that our twins will probably be premature. How early should we expect them?

The average length of pregnancy for twins is thirty-seven weeks, for triplets thirty-five weeks and for quadruplets thirty-four weeks. But this is only the average length; about a quarter of twin pregnancies are shorter than thirty-seven weeks.

My husband says that we have identical twins because there is a history of twins in his family, but I've heard that they can only be passed down through the mother. Which of us is right?

It is very rare for MZ twins to be hereditary, so it is unlikely that either of you is right. However, DZ twins do run in families, but only through the mother, and if you already have one set of DZ twins then you are much more likely to have a second set. There is no evidence to support the theory that twins always skip a generation. If your parents had DZ twins, then you are just as likely to have a pair as your children.

I'm expecting twins, but I've been told that there is a greater risk of losing one of twins than a single baby. Is that right?

There is a slightly greater mortality risk for twins both before and after birth, but the care and treatment of mothers and babies is improving all the time.

It is important to follow the doctor's recommendations and take as much rest as possible. Standing around is not recommended but a light folding chair is quite easy to take with you if you think you may need one. 'Eating for three' means making sure that you have a good balanced diet with plenty of fresh fruit and vegetables. You may put on a little extra weight, but this is quite normal. Give up smoking, at least during the pregnancy, as this will give your babies a better chance. Have regular checkups.

Expect two healthy babies and there is a high probability that that is exactly what you will get. Don't blame yourself if one does not survive. Nature is performing something of a conjuring trick, and she occasionally gets it wrong.

I've just stopped taking the pill because I'd like to start a family. Does having taken the pill increase or decrease the likelihood of my having twins?

The experts do not seem to be in total agreement over this. But there is a possibility that at the moment you have a slightly increased chance of having identical twins but, unless you conceive quite quickly, your chances of having twins becomes less.

Our twins are so alike and yet they are not identical. We've heard about a third type of twin and wondered if that was what ours are?

A lot of non-identical twins are very alike, just as two brothers or sisters can sometimes look extraordinarily alike. But it has been discovered that there is a third type of twin which is mother identical, father non-identical. In other words the egg splits before fertilization, by two separate sperms, takes place. It is almost impossible to determine the precentage of such twins in the twin population, but they would be fairly rare.

What do you think of the idea of having the second twin implanted one year after the first?

In vitro fertilized eggs cannot be identical unless they split after implantation, in which case they would be born together. So we are talking about non-identical twins. Such children, therefore, will be just like any other brothers or sisters, but would have lost the opportunity of learning to share with another of their own age and of having the extra companionship that comes with being a twin.

It is very likely that, with only a year between them, they will still be close, but a single fetus will have a better start and should go to full term. After the births the mother can give each baby individual love and attention and there will be less opportunity for comparison between them.

Parents would have to be quite firm if one of the twins complained about his position in the family. They are lucky to have parents who have worked especially hard to bring them into the world, and there are advantages and disadvantages about every position in the family. Children need simple straightforward answers without long-drawn-out explanations. In adolescence children have a way of homing-in on their parents' uncertainties, so it is best if these have been discussed between the parents without the children being present. Parents can then support each other in giving matter-of-fact and honest answers to their children's questions, without allowing the subject to become a way of gaining negative attention. (See 'Parenting' sections.)

We're expecting twins and feeling rather anxious about coping with two new babies, let alone how we're going to afford two of everything. Where can we go for help?

Ask at your antenatal clinic for the address of your local twins club or write to your national association (see page 167). They will usually put you in touch with parents of twins to whom you can talk about your fears. The local clubs may know where there is a second-hand pram or buggy for sale and may also be able to give you the names of shops who offer a discount to parents of twins.

I still have a definite preference for one of my twins and feel very guilty although I have told no one about it. What should I do?

Preferences often persist so don't feel guilty about it. If they are both healthy, happy babies you may find that reading the chapter on parenting (page 46) will give you tips on how to maintain a good relationship with both twins. Occasionally the less-preferred twin can be a particularly vulnerable baby and, in spite of the mother's efforts, make her feel that she is failing with him. Your health visitor or doctor are the best source of help in these situations.

I would like to breast-feed my twins. Where can I go for advice?

Ask your local twins club for an excellent leaflet called 'Breast-feeding Twins' or send away for a copy to your national association (see page 167).

The older child

How does the arrival of twins affect the older brother or sister? The younger they are, often the more easily they adjust, but there are no hard and fast rules. It does seem to be more difficult to adjust to the arrival of two small brothers or sisters than one. Twins require more attention from the parents and attract more attention from other adults. From being the star attraction, the older sibling is forced to retire to the back row of the chorus! However, parents often find that they have a closer bond with the older child than with the twins, though he may not be as cuddly, which is not surprising considering the competition.

Boys seem to find it rather more difficult to cope with younger twins than girls, perhaps because girls have ways of remaining centre-stage, but it may also be because the relationship with the opposite sex parent, i.e. father, does not change very much. Little girls are often very good at copying their mothers and may be a useful extra pair of hands, but they can also be clingy and demanding. A jealous little boy is more likely to act out physically and start a vicious circle of irritation and bad behaviour.

How can the older child best be helped to cope with the new arrivals? If the mother has been away from home in hospital for more than two or three days, the toddler will usually be demanding and attention-seeking on her return and may not let her out of his sight. If this need for reassurance is accepted and respected and there are plenty of cuddles whilst the new twins are sleeping, he should gradually settle down. However, although small allowances need to be made so that he feels secure in the parents' love for him, it is still important for him to feel safe in the knowledge that his parents are in charge and that the house rules have remained the same.

Toddlers can adapt fairly quickly to a routine, and, though demand feeding may be rewarding and helpful for twins on their own or where there are much older brothers or sisters, it can be much easier to organize the older toddler if feed times are fairly predictable. It's very difficult for him to sit through hours of breast or bottle-feeding small babies, and if he can be persuaded to have a rest during at least one of them the parent can enjoy it more, and give him time later. Perhaps he could spend an hour with a neighbour if he doesn't have a rest. If it's at the same time as a children's television programme, he may watch it quite happily, if he doesn't feel he should be putting on his own performance for the benefit of his mother.

A special box of toys which the older child can play with whilst his mother is feeding the twins can also be helpful. New items can be added and old ones removed. The contents need not be expensive: clothes pegs, jam-jar lids and cotton reels are just as interesting to a toddler. Items for the older child can be picked up at jumble sales. He will learn to look forward to 'special box' times. When the box is put away he can be rewarded with some special attention for himself and told how good he's been.

Parents tend to have an expectation of sympathetic understanding from the older child: 'Why doesn't he realize that I have my hands full and go and play on his own?' He often does understand only too well, but it may make him more resentful rather than co-operative and he can show it by an increase in temper tantrums. By contrast with the twins, the older child can seem more grown up than he really is and he may try to live up to the parents' expectations. However, sometimes he can find it difficult and may try to be a baby again like the twins. It might be his toilet training that goes out of the window or he reverts to baby-talk and bouts of temper.

A mother with one or two babies on her lap will often simply sit and shout at the older child in the hope of making him stop whatever it is that he is doing – getting up seems to require so much effort. It usually has the opposite effect. The child succeeds in getting his mother's attention and continues misbehaving. This only makes the mother more angry and frustrated. Fathers can also fall into the same trap. In the long run it can be quicker and less effort to put the baby or babies on the floor for a few seconds and deal with the older child, or, instead of shouting, to point out something else that might interest him and distract his attention. Parents need to mean what they say. If they don't mean it, it's better left unsaid.

If left unchecked but continually told that he's naughty, the older child may come to believe it and feel that goodness is beyond his reach. If, right from the beginning, he is helped to see himself as basically good and given plenty of praise whenever he behaves as the parent would like him to, many later difficulties can be avoided and a good family relationship built up.

Most of the tips on parenting twins can be used with the older brother or sister to advantage. Little boys, like little girls, can be encouraged to help and feel important and twins can often bring out very loving and caring qualities in the older child.

We all need some space and the older child needs his space as well to play with his toys without 'help' from the twins. Once twins are on the move, a playpen can be useful, so that they can play with their toys and the older child with his, without having his game spoiled. It can also be a help for busy mothers who can safely leave the room for five minutes knowing that the twins will come to no harm. In the early days it can be used to contain the twins' carrycots to keep them safe from the prying hands of the over-inquisitive toddler. Some parents may prefer to use the play-pen as the older child's space as he is able to climb in and out as he wishes and the twins are then free to explore a wider territory.

Once twins have mastered the art of climbing they can be taught that a particular corner of the room belongs to the older child, perhaps a couple of cardboard boxes or chairs can be used to form a boundary. If the dog is entitled to sanctuary in his basket, then the older child is entitled to sanctuary too! If he has a bedroom of his own, he will begin to use this for games with his friends, and special projects, as he grows more independent.

The older child will be able to have a little time with his parents after the twins have gone to bed, and he can have a game and a chat and some special attention for himself. It is all too easy to switch on the television, but, though he may enjoy watching it, the opportunity is being missed for parents and child to get to know each other. If it is at all possible to take him out occasionally with one parent or, even better, both, he will probably be a little angel, rather than a nuisance, and enjoy being with the grown-ups. If there are several older children, they will all benefit from a special time for themselves, and different bedtimes can be a useful way of achieving this. In larger families occasional outings with each child on his own, even if it's only to the shops with, perhaps, time for coffee or a Coke, will help parents to maintain an individual relationship with all the children. This will increase the children's sense of personal worth and value.

Children vary, as we do ourselves, and their tolerance of new situations will depend very much on their own past experience as well as their own make-up and that of the twins. The best way that parents can help them is to give them as much love and interest as time will permit, within a secure framework in which to grow and learn.

If, in spite of their efforts, a child begins to behave in a way that is disrupting the family or that gives cause for concern, it is much better to seek early professional support than wait and allow a relatively small difficulty become a major one. Just talking to someone else about a problem can be an enormous relief in itself.

How can I best prepare our child for the arrival of twins?

It is wise not to tell him too soon; very early diagnosis does not guarantee the birth of twins. Also young children have a very hazy sense of time and may expect the twins to arrive the next day. Once the bulge has become obvious then it is time to tell the curious toddler, particularly as twins have a habit of arriving early.

A visit to another mother who already has twins might be arranged through your health visitor or local twins club, so that the youngster can see for himself what is in store, and so can you. It is better not to tell him that he is going to have twin brothers or sisters because he has been a 'good boy', as if there are any birth complications he may blame himself for not having been good enough. If a visit to see baby twins can't be arranged, then pictures are a good substitute and they are available to be looked at at any time. It's also helpful to tell him that new babies are very tiny and sleepy, so they won't be able to play with him until they grow a little bigger. They will be very pleased to have a big brother, or sister, to help mummy and daddy look after them.

Too many changes at once are difficult for the toddler to handle, so if he is due to go to playgroup or nursery school soon after the twins are born, it can be useful to start him about three months before the twins are due, if this is possible. He can then settle in and not feel pushed out by the twins. If he is too young, then a delay in starting time can be helpful. A child who is already at playgroup may become tearful and clingy again after the twins are born, but this generally does not last very long. He will be much happier at playgroup than having to try and occupy himself all day at home whilst you're busy with the twins. There may even be more time for him if you've had a chance to do some of the housework while he's been occupied, though most parents find that the time between taking and fetching is all too short.

My three-year-old little girl never leaves the twins alone and every time they go to sleep she wakes them up. I can't get on with anything.

She may think that you are so busy that this is the only way to get your attention. Of course she doesn't realize that it just makes you busier still. A reward system is probably the best method for dealing with this type of situation. Tell her that if she doesn't wake up the twins you will read her a story or play a game with her before the twins have their next feed, but that if she wakes them up there will be no playtime. If you see her about to poke the twins you can remind her of the bargain. Small children find it difficult to wait for a reward until the end of the day, so the day needs to be broken up into small sections each of which can earn the reward. It can be useful to watch her every move at the start of the new system, or make the period of time very short so that she can earn the reward and be praised for it and learn how the system works. If she wakes the twins, they get the attention and she is treated quite normally with no extra attention at all, not even a reprimand, and of course no special playtime.

Trying to keep up with the housework is almost impossible for the mother of twins. Accept any offers of help and reduce the ironing to the minimum. Encourage your little girl to help, too. It may take longer but at least it will be more enjoyable.

My little boy keeps biting and scratching the twins. How do I stop him? It's worrying me so much that they spend most of the time in their room where he can't get at them.

He's found a way of getting plenty of attention and he probably also feels quite angry with the twins. It's important for him to learn that he does not have the power to remove the twins, but that he will be the one to go to his room if he attacks them. If he is given one warning then removed to his room for five minutes on each occasion that he hurts the twins, he should get the message.

A reward system, like the one above, will also help him to gain attention for the right reasons rather than for the wrong ones. Do give him plenty of praise when he leaves the twins alone.

All older children need a special time for themselves before they go to bed, and praise if they've been playing quietly on their own.

My older child has reverted to soiling. What should I do?

It's best to ignore it and just clean up the mess. Praise him when he uses his potty or the toilet. It could be that now you have the twins he is expected to go to the toilet on his own and he is not quite ready for this. If all his toilet training has been forgotten, it may be preferable to allow him to return to nappies and wait a few months before toilet training again.

I think my older child may be hyperactive. He used to be quite a placid baby, but now he's forever on the go. I find him quite exhausting, and he simply won't do as I ask him.

It's quite a good idea to stand up next to your toddler and then ask yourself who should really be in charge. Take back the control, and you should find that he won't be quite so constantly on the go. Under 'Parenting' (page 46) you may find some ideas that will help you to restore the balance.

Every mealtime is a misery. My older child refuses to eat anything unless we feed him every mouthful and takes hours over eating a small portion of food. My husband and I are both tired at the end of the day and quickly run out of patience. My husband insists that he eats everything on his plate and sometimes he's still sitting at the table after we have got down.

Your child has succeeded in hitting you where it hurts most – in the heart! No parent wants to see his child starve or see the food that has been worked for and lovingly prepared almost literally thrown back in his face.

Your child is managing to get a great deal of attention and some of the babying that he's been missing since the arrival of the twins.

If it's possible it might be better, until he's a little older, for him to have his main meal in the middle of the day and for you to have your meal a little later after he has had a snack and gone to bed. At lunchtime you should both be less tired and parents deserve some peace and quiet at the end of the day. If this is not possible, then both parents need to prepare a joint strategy. First mentally knock a year off your child's age and treat him accordingly. Stick to small portions (he can always come back for more) and tell him that if he eats it all up you will give him a nice jelly, yogurt, or whatever it is that you know he likes. A dessert always used to be the carrot that made it worth while eating the less interesting part of the meal, but it seems to have been neglected in recent times.

Refuse to be irritated by any bids for negative attention, but give him lots of praise for good behaviour. Any tantrums and he goes to his room with the minimum of fuss until you have finished eating; he won't come to any harm if he misses the occasional meal, and he'll make it up the next day anyway. But if he still gets a snack before he goes to bed, the reward system will not work. Avoid biscuits and drinks just before mealtimes as these may spoil his appetite.

All children, like adults, have pet hates and these should be respected, but if they change from day to day then you will know that they are bids for attention.

My older child keeps rocking himself, sometimes in a chair but often when he is in his bed; we can hear the noise of the bed banging at night. Often he is fast asleep and doesn't know he is doing it.

Ignore the behaviour as much as possible and offer distractions. If he is not already going to a playgroup then it would be very helpful if he could join one. If finances are short your health visitor may be able to assist in finding a place in a local authority nursery. Encourage other children to come into the house to play with him and take the children out as much as possible. Chat to him whilst the twins are in their pram or pushchair. 'Good' children can often be ignored, so keep talking to him when you're doing other things and take an interest in his play. A special time just for him will also help.

Yes, but what about. . . .

There will be some more questions and answers at the end of the section on older siblings of five to eleven, some of which may also apply to the top end of the under fives. The chapters on parenting twins may also help to answer some of your questions.

4
Identity

Right from the beginning the identical twin has more difficulty in establishing his independent identity. He recognizes his twin in the mirror before he recognizes himself and is three months behind the non-identical twin in recognizing his own mirror image. He takes longer to say 'I' and 'me' and more often answers to his twin's name. It is probable that the look-alike non-identicals have the same problem.

Dorothy Burlingham, in one of the earliest studies of twin children, remarked on the reaction of other small children to the twins and how often they behaved as if the children were interchangeable. One child got very cross when twin Peter refused to answer when called 'other Paul', and triplets suffered from the same treatment.

Parents sometimes lose the original hospital nametags and may re-allocate names when consistent small differences enable them to be sure which one is which.

The human infant takes a long time before he is physically able to do things independently of his mother and for this reason his early sense of identity includes that relationship. Gradually, as he learns to crawl and walk, he discovers that he has an identity that is separate from his mother, that, for a short time at least, he can explore the world on his own without coming to any harm. Games of beep-bo help him to learn that a temporary disappearance of mother is always followed by her return, and a special toy or piece of cloth may act as a mother substitute when she is not there. Gradually he builds up his own personal identikit picture based on clues from the world around him.

If the infant is one of twins then he may feel equally uncomfortable at first when his twin is not close by. As the weeks pass he may find that his twin is more reliably around than his mother. He discovers he has a separate identity from her, but he may feel that this identity still includes his twin, particularly when the outside world reacts to them as though they were one person.

Never having had the security of being able to command his mother's entire attention, he may be less willing to let her go unless his twin is with him. Not only does this give him an extra sense of security, but also makes sure that his twin is not getting the attention that he himself is missing. Jealousy is an emotion that twins probably experience earlier than other children, and for this reason it may be particularly strong.

Twins usually try to find ways of avoiding situations that can create jealousy. Identical twins, because of their strong identification with each other, find it very difficult to tolerate such feelings. To avoid jealousy twins may each attach themselves to a different parent and play out the parents' roles within their own partnership. This can often be seen in the under-fives when one takes on the maternal, caring role in their relationship, tucking the other one into bed perhaps, or making sure that he has his coat on before they go out to play. The other twin may act as his twin's protector, fighting their joint battles. Choice of roles may be influenced by the children's early emotional and physical make-up and is more likely to change in the case of identical twins where these differences are smaller. Other ways of avoiding jealousy are to always have the same as each other and to be as alike as possible.

The relationship is such a close one in the early years that a toddler who is separated from his twin, perhaps by a period in hospital, may react in a very similar way to that of a child separated from his mother. His feelings are so strong that he cuts himself off from emotion and rejects the loved object that he feels has rejected him. Visits by the twin will help to reassure him, even if he appears to react badly to them. On his return, allowances may need to be made for anger directed towards the twin as well as towards the parent. This is also a way of testing out the relationship and the twin will often show a great deal of understanding.

So, because they are together so much, because they may look alike, because they are often treated as interchangeable, or as two parts of a whole, and because the separation from mother may be incomplete, twins do not go through the same steps as most single children in acquiring a sense of personal identity and self-sufficiency. How can we help them to achieve independence and confidence in the first few years?

If twins of any type are to be their own person, they need to be treated as two separate individuals rather than one of a pair. Small twins do look delightful when they're dressed alike, but they look equally sweet dressed in different colours. If they have their own set of colours it can become a visual shorthand, even if they have their backs turned – if he's wearing a red sweater it must be John. John himself will be able to tell at a glance if he looks in the mirror. As soon as practicable, individual wardrobes will help to build up their personal identity.

The easiest way to make twins look different is to cut or style their hair differently. This can enable twins who would usually be impossible to tell apart to be instantly recognizable by friends and relatives. Though most parents can tell their identical twins apart if they look carefully, it's being able to tell at a glance that's important.

Opportunities for parents to get to know their twins individually help to create a separate sense of identity and to build up a normal relationship with the parents. This can help to avoid an over-dependence on the twin.

Mothers of twins may often feel that no one else can manage two at a time, or that it is trespassing too much on their good nature to ask others to look after twins whilst they go shopping and so on. The answer could be to leave one of the twins and take the other. Shopping with both twins can be a strain, but it is surprising how much easier it can be with only one, even when there is an older child as well. Each twin could take it in turns to be left with someone else so that they both get the advantage of the extra attention that the mother can give them. Hopefully, the twin who is left behind is also getting some individual attention. Fathers, too, might feel more secure and develop greater confidence in looking after infant twins if they are only left with one at a time. Again it's important that twins take it in turns to be with their father.

Time that mothers spend at home with each twin is valuable as well. Twins may have a different daytime sleeping pattern so that opportunities occur naturally for separate playtimes. If they are not so obliging, grandparents and neighbours can help by amusing one twin for a little while whilst the mother plays with the other. There can be a temptation to give the less-preferred twin to someone else and play with the more rewarding one, or even, in an attempt to adjust the balance, to do it the other way round. Time with both twins is the best way, but it sometimes helps to take each twin into another room to play so that comparisons cannot be made.

Another way in which we can reinforce the twins' sense of personal identity is to treat them as individuals at birthdays and Christmas. It seems so much easier to make birthdays a joint affair that many parents forget that it's almost as quick to make two cakes as one. Then each child can blow out his own candles and cut his own cake. Getting used to having separate, and different, birthday and christmas presents at an early age, even if they insist on both playing with one of them, can introduce them to a sense of life offering them individual choices and possibilities. This will help to prevent the struggle to be the same that parents often experience with older twins that can be difficult to resist.

It is a good idea to give each twin his own toys in his own box so that they don't have to share unless they wish to. It's their own personal property. This will prevent screaming to claim ownership and encourage real sharing, which means allowing someone else to share what belongs to you.

We've been given so many presents of matching clothes, we can't afford to throw them all away.

Pass the word around that you've decided you are going to dress your twins differently from now on and try mix-and-matching. For the time being you could sew individual labels on to the clothes, or maybe there's a granny or aunt who does embroidery. Labels can always be helpful, even when twins are dressed differently as names can get mixed up.

My twins refuse to be dressed differently; does it really matter?

Only you can decide that, but it's possible that your twins have got used to being dressed the same way and don't feel very confident about being different. If you would like them to be dressed differently, you could perhaps introduce them to the idea of having different colours for the same items. It may be better to allow them to keep the matching clothes that they already have, and introduce new ones as they grow out of them.

If the twins are non-identical, what will suit one will not necessarily suit the other, so it will be easier to dress them differently. If, as I suspect, they are identical, they may be happier in similar clothes, but like teenagers, who all tend to dress alike, there can be many variations on the same theme. All children are by nature conservative, particularly when they are little, but they will gradually get used to dressing differently. At this age the decision has to be yours.

I don't understand why twins should be dressed differently. Twins are special and have a special relationship, particularly identical twins, and like to be the same.

You're quite right, identical twins do have a natural wish to be the same and tend to make the same choices, but read through the book and you may find some reasons for encouraging them to go along different, though perhaps parallel, paths.

We would like to give our twins a tricycle each for their fourth birthday. How can we give each of them something different?

Of course you can't. Just as some other big items, a doll's house for example, may have to be shared. The answer on these occasions could be to give each child a small personal gift as well.

My husband works long hours and is only at home with the children on Sundays and we like to have time together as a family. We have no relations living near to help us. How can I get time on my own with the babies?

It may be difficult whilst they are very small, but don't discourage your neighbours' older children from coming in to play with the babies, under your supervision of course. They can be excellent nursemaids and will talk to the twins. A grateful neighbour may be more inclined to mind one of the babies for you occasionally. Do contact the local twins club for extra support.

If we don't give our twins exactly the same, they both sit and cry until we do or fight between themselves. It saves so much trouble to give in to them. Should we change?

It is almost impossible to be always equal and if your twins learn that joint pressure will make you change your mind, you are going to have a very powerful pair of twins. Trouble avoided now may mean more trouble in store for you later. Don't let your twins make you doubt your ability to parent. Work with your partner so that you are not outnumbered, and start as you mean to go on. It's surprising how quickly the under-fives will accept that the double act is not working any more. If parents are seen to be firm, but fair, their judgement will be respected and impossible demands will not be made either of them or others in the twins' lives.

We have mixed-sex twins. Our little boy loves to play with his sister's dolls and is a very gentle soul. She prefers his cars.

We're a bit worried that he's going to be called a sissy when he goes to school.

Boys from mixed-sex pairs are just as masculine as any other boys, but tend not to be as macho. Being so much with his sister, who may be a little bossy, he is influenced by her, just as she is by him. Separate playgroup or nursery school will help them both to be themselves, and is particularly important for mixed-sex twins where the girl can become the boy's 'social secretary'. Your son will also benefit from doing things with dad without his sister, whilst Mother and daughter have some time together. Don't worry. One day he'll make someone a very nice husband.

5
Language Development

Why should language development in twins be any different from that of single children?

The answer is that there would be no difference if the twins were separated within the first few months and brought up separately. We know this because such twins have been found and tested on their verbal IQ and the results are similar to those of single children. Why should it be different when twins are brought up together?

There are several reasons. First, busy and tired mothers tend to talk less to their small children whether they are twins or part of a closely spaced family. Second, parents of twins tend to talk to them as a pair rather than separately, for example: 'John and David would you like me to read you a story?' It's not only parents who fall into this trap, so do granny and grandpa, the playgroup teacher, the lady next door and the postman. Although it has been shown that mothers of twins talk nearly as much to twins as they do to a single child, it has to be shared between them and pre-school twins are less likely to ask questions or address remarks to adults than single children. Lastly twins spend a great deal of time playing and talking to each other, so that they reinforce each other's mistakes and have less opportunity of learning new verbal skills.

One of the side effects is the development of a private language know as 'ideoglossia' which is often unintelligible to other members of the family. Over forty per cent of all twins develop a private language when they are at the toddler stage, though it is slightly more common among boys than girls, and among identical twins than non-identical twins. Occasionally it can occur in very closely spaced single children. It's not really a different language at all, it's based on at least ninety per cent of the parents' vocabulary and it's not intended to be secret. However, slightly older children may discover that using it is a way of hiding their conversation from outsiders, rather like using backslang. The odd baby word can be interpreted in the context of a situation or sentence, but the use of several in a row can prove baffling. Here is an example from one set of English twins:

Did odo beer
Lizzy goes to school

The particular disadvantage is that there is no sentence construction and there is a free word order, with the most important word coming first. This may delay the learning of verbal skills. Most children grow out of it by the time they start first school.

Although twins have a slightly lower average IQ score than single children on verbal tests, they may have a higher one on non-verbal tests. In other words, they develop compensatory skills. Most twins do a lot of catching up once they go to first school.

Verbal skills are clearly important for learning, so how can we best help twins to develop their language ability in the pre-school years?

First, parents should try to speak to each child individually and encourage others to do the same. Watch out for the twin who acts as spokesman for the pair: twins may be happy to divide their roles in this way, but one twin is getting less opportunity to develop his language and social skills. Second, if possible, send the twins to playgroup on alternate days, both together on Fridays to give the parents a break. Not only will this encourage them to learn to talk to other children and adults, but it will also help them to gain confidence in doing things on their own and reinforce their sense of identity. Whilst one child is at playgroup or nursery school, the other child is able to enjoy more of the parents' time and attention and is also developing his language skills at the same time. It's a great opportunity for parents to get to know their twins individually on a regular basis. Finally for twins, as for all children, familiarity with books provides an incentive to learning, and bedtime, or anytime, stories open up the world of imagination.

We can't afford the local playgroup more than twice a week. Should we just send the twins one day each?

Unless you're getting a reduction for quantity, you should double up the number of days that you have one twin at playgroup if you send them one at a time. In other words two days for both means four days when you send only one, which may make life a little easier for you. However if you mean that they can both go only once each, then yes, even just one day on their own is invaluable.

Our playgroup insists that parents come in and help and I'm expected to come in twice as often because I have two children attending. How can I get time with the twins on my own?

If you only send one at a time, it's as though you only have one child at playgroup, so hopefully this arrangement will enable you to cut down on the amount of time you spend helping. Parents of twins may feel that they have to put a brave face on and not admit that sometimes it's hard to cope. For some parents, particularly those with triplets and quads, the children may be the result of treatment for infertility and it can be hinted that parents have brought their troubles upon themselves. Don't be intimidated. Make it clear that you're very willing to help, but on the same basis as the other mothers; there's only one of you although you have doubled up on the children. It's surprising how understanding other people can be if you are honest with them.

Our twins are three but their speech is not as clear as our friends' children and other people have difficulty in understanding them. Will they grow out of it?

Let your health visitor or doctor know that you are worried and ask if you could have an appointment with a speech therapist. The speech therapist sees many small children and can give you excellent advice and help if necessary. The earlier that children are seen the better. Some of the tips contained in this section will also help to improve their speech.

Our twins have a private language of their own. Will they be very behind at school?

Nearly half of all twins have their own language and, though there is some association with slightly poorer language ability, there is no reason why they should not do well at school, although they may have a little catching up to do. Do follow the tips contained in this section and if you are worried about their speech have a talk with your health visitor or doctor.

I tried sending them to playgroup separately, but they cried so much that I gave up. Should I try again?

All children find it difficult to separate, and many mothers have left tearful children at playgroup who have settled down quite quickly once they've gone. Find out from the playgroup teacher how long it takes each child to settle. If the time gets progressively shorter, you're winning, though in reality it is the children who have a great deal to gain.

Having given in once it may take a little longer before the twins are convinced that you are not going to change your mind for a second time. However, only you know your twins and if they are very distressed, or things at home are going through a bad patch for some reason, they will get extra security from being together and separation can be delayed until later when the time is right. Moving house or a relative dying are examples of home situations that may affect twins, as they will a single child, because they affect the whole family.

My problem is not with the twin whose day it is to go to playgroup, it's with the one who has to stay at home. I think they'd rather be with their twin than with me.

They may well think they're missing something special that the twin is getting at playgroup, particularly if they enjoy the experience. The answer is to make being at home special too. It can be a good idea to have some play material so that they can have their own mini-playschool at home, and for them to have some time when they can be sure of getting all your attention. You may find that they start crying to stay home instead!

My little girl has made lots of friends at playgroup and is invited to lots of parties, but her twin brother seems to have no friends at all.

Perhaps this can be turned to advantage: it might give him some extra time with his father when his sister is not around, to do some of the things that little boys like doing – preventing his father from mending the car or digging the garden, kicking a ball around, or just having the chance to be with his father on his own. The important thing is not to worry about it. Little girls tend to be more sociable than little boys and to have more parties.

Going to playgroup on separate days, if they're not doing so already, is particularly helpful for mixed-sex twins as little girls tend to take charge when they are together. The boy will learn how to make friends on his own and become more confident and the girl won't feel that she's always got to be looking after him, though with some mixed-sex twins it can be the other way round.

We have triplets. We can't possibly send them to nursery school on different days.

Why not send two at a time, leaving one at home, changing the pairs each day, and perhaps sending them all together twice a week? This will help to prevent one triplet becoming the odd one out and give you the time with each one that is so difficult to find with triplets.

6
Parenting

Is 'Double Trouble' fact or fiction? Double trouble is a bit like the Terrible Twos, 'two' here meaning the age and not the number of children. Some children are naturally biddable, never touch anything that they are not supposed to touch, sleep peacefully all night and wake at a respectable hour in the morning. Others demand attention from the moment they get up, need watching every minute of the day, keep their parents awake all night and are ready for off at five o'clock in the morning. Amazingly both types of children can be born to the same parents and sometimes at the same time!

The 'twos' are not necessarily 'terrible' any more than twins are necessarily double trouble. Twins can often be less trouble because they are not totally dependent on the parents for amusement, and if one twin has got up on the wrong side of the bed, the other twin may provide all the soothing that is needed.

Twins, like other children, are individuals and generally behave in an individual way, but sometimes parents may find that they have two of a kind. They may be two angelic children or two exhausting children, and this doesn't only apply to identical twins.

If both twins get on top of a parent, possibly literally, the parent may hesitate to take a firm line because there are two of them and only one of him. Two parents working together can make all the difference, but both parents may not always be available. Left unchecked, the behaviour gets worse, just as it would if there were only one child, but, because there are two, the parent starts to blame himself. Is he providing what they need? Guilt can make a parent feel helpless.

This chapter does not contain all the answers, but it attempts to deal with some of the problems that parents may meet. Ways of avoiding possible pitfalls and, hopefully, some of those moments of self doubt, are suggested.

POO

Time

Giving children time is important, but they cannot have the parents' attention on demand. Even a toddler can learn to wait, but he needs to know that there are certain times of the day when he will receive his parents' undivided attention.

Although, on the face of it, twins are more able to amuse themselves than single children, twins under five should not be left playing on their own too long. When bored they can become destructive and aggressive, just like any other small children. For these times it's useful to have a cupboard with some playschool-type materials. Here are some ideas to choose from:

Blunt scissors
Colouring and cut-out books
Paper
Crayons
Stiff card
Paints for older children
Plasticine or play-doh
Paper glue
Coloured paper
Old Christmas cards
Left-over knitting wool

All these are best kept well out of the reach of children. They can be very imaginative in the use of paints, glue, crayons, scissors etc. when no-one is looking.

Children can sit with their parents around the kitchen table, or on newspaper on the floor, and everyone can be involved in creative playtime. Time spent at the table needs to be graded to the children's attention span. It can be increased as the children grow older and can concentrate longer. When parents are involved, children play better, but once children have lost interest they will usually become silly and instead of enjoying the time spent it will become a source of irritation for everyone. No one will feel like repeating the experience. 'Stop while you're winning' is a good motto.

Because twins often require more organizational skills than single children, they can find it difficult to organize themselves. This may lead to pressure on the parents to decide who does what when, and every small difference is taken to arbitration. Most under-fives will sort out their own differences if parents leave them to it. If the crescendo of small raised voices does not bring the parent running, they will probably give up and turn to something else that they can both agree on. If, however, they are bent on battle, distraction rather than arbitration may be a better way of dealing with the situation.

Consistency

Consistency is an important ingredient in parenting all children, but is particularly important when the children are twins. If parents are tired there is a temptation to leave children to it, even if they are doing something that is usually not allowed. This is a short-sighted policy. If rules are to be developed, for example about objects that can be touched and objects that can't be touched, then the rules need to apply on all occasions. If parents keep changing their minds, then the children will take no notice.

It's a good idea to place all but essential items out of the toddlers' reach in order to avoid a constant stream of 'nos'. If a toddler is distracted or offered alternative play material on each and every occasion that he reaches for a forbidden object, he should eventually learn to resist the temptation. He will understand that 'no' means 'no' if 'no' doesn't sometimes mean 'yes'. Parents need to work together; one saying 'no' and the other 'yes' is a recipe for disaster. The rule of divide and conquer is one that twins, like all children, quickly learn. If an object is not too precious, it can be helpful to satisfy the toddler's curiosity by letting him touch it and feel it, sitting down under the watchful eye of the parent. It is then replaced and the child's interest usually transfers to something else. 'No' has been avoided and the child has learned something new about the world around him.

Consistency not only means parents sticking to the rules about what may or may not be touched, but also about bedtimes, jumping on the furniture, taking off muddy wellies by the back door, biscuits before mealtimes, whatever the house rules are. There will be different rules for different families.

As soon as the children do as they are asked, they should be told that they are a good boy or good girl. Toddlers quite enjoy a round of applause!

Negative attention

Children like to attract their parents' attention and twins are no exception. If they find that a particular piece of behaviour persuades the parents to stop whatever it is that they are doing and concentrate on them, then they will keep repeating it. It doesn't seem to matter whether the attention is positive or negative. There are degrees of negative attention, from nagging, through to shouting, smacking and finally having 'the screaming habdabs' where the parents' attention is totally on the child or children. A list of some of the behaviours which could provoke negative attention might be:

Using naughty words
Jumping on the furniture
Climbing on top of the cupboard
Throwing food on the floor
Racing round the room at top speed
Whining
Playing with the genital area
Squabbling
Refusing to pick up toys
Crying
Having a tantrum
Not getting dressed/undressed
Head-banging
Wetting
Soiling
Biting

but there will also be particular forms of behaviour that are individually tailored to the parents' own special requirements.

The tantrum is probably the most popular way of getting negative attention and seems to work on almost any parent. As twins have a tendency to specialize, if one twin corners the market in tantrums the other twin may not bother.

What is the best way of dealing with a tantrum? First check to see if there is an easy solution to the bout of frustration, for example by encouraging the child to succeed in something that he lacks confidence in doing. If this fails, try distraction. If the tantrum is aimed at making parents say 'yes', instead of 'no', stick to your guns and allow the child to have his tantrum without any extra outside help. If parents start shouting too, or getting angry, then this may provide the child with another reason for having a tantrum – getting his parents' attention. If he doesn't succeed in getting this attention, then he has one less reason for having a tantrum. If he's one of twins, his co-twin may then feel he's entitled to one or two himself, which is much better than always bottling things up. All toddlers have angry feelings sometimes and if we're not frightened by them, we can help the toddler not to feel frightened either.

A playpen is an important piece of equipment for twin babies, but parents are advised not to pass it on to someone else too soon as it could be needed again. No, not for the next baby (though of course that's always a possibility), but for occasions when both twins misbehave at the same time. The parent should remain by the playpen, so that the twins don't climb out, and as soon as one or both have calmed down, they are allowed out with plenty of praise. If they misbehave again, they are put back in the playpen until they get the message. If a successful toddler receives a round of applause he will usually learn more quickly.

As they get older a few minutes' cooling off in their bedroom can be helpful, but always the praise when they come out, tantrum over. If both twins have a tantrum, both can be sent to their bedroom. If they start playing happily together, well, that was the intention in the first place. Check for mischief, and if all is well they can be told how pleased the parents are with each of them and that they may come down whenever they would like to. The toddler can sometimes benefit from having time out in his room as well, particularly if the parents' patience is stretched to breaking point and they are in need of some space, but again, only for a few minutes.

A problem can arise when one twin starts to cry or become upset simply because his co-twin is doing so. He may also get angry with his parents because they seem to be responsible for his twin's unhappiness. This can make parents feel unsure of themselves –

are they being too severe? Or they may retreat in the face of overwhelming odds. Parents should concentrate on the original culprit, whilst reassuring his twin that 'John will stop crying in a minute', and weather the storm. Identical twins, in particular, tend to identify with the mood of the other, but the quicker the situation is dealt with the quicker the incident is over. The plus side is that twins who react to each other's unhappy feelings, will also identify with the happy ones.

If we look at the behaviour list, we can see that some are in italics and some aren't. All the behaviours may have started out innocently enough, but those in italics are encouraged by negative attention alone, whilst the other behaviours are also encouraged by parents being uncertain about saying 'no', or not having discovered the 'one-warning system' (see below).

The child who uses 'naughty words' is only repeating what he has overheard, from another child perhaps, and has no idea that they are naughty until his parents get cross. If he's ignored when he says them, or parents pretend not to understand, he will soon find some 'good' ones to use instead.

The behaviours on the list which are in italics may sometimes be caused or increased by stress, for example a new baby in the family, starting playgroup, overtiredness or moving home. A child may also identify with his parents' feelings if they are under stress. If parents react in an undisturbed way when the behaviour occurs and offer distraction when possible, the child will find it less rewarding.

Playing with the genital area is quite normal in young children, but if parents find it embarrassing, jeans and romp suits can make the genital area slightly less accessible than dresses and short trousers.

The parents' worry that the child will hurt himself can act as a great incentive to the head-banger. It's best to ignore him and transfer attention to the other child. He may soon be tempted to find out what is going on and join in. However if ignoring the habit doesn't result in a reduction after a week, it's best to ask for advice from the doctor or health visitor. Don't wait to go to the doctor if the child has other worrying symptoms.

In the case of toilet training, attention needs to be concentrated on successes, rather than failures.

The fear that one child will be hurt may cause anxiety and over-reaction when one or both twins are biters. Biting is a quite natural form of behaviour for babies and toddlers but can get out of hand, particularly if it attracts attention from the adults. Toddler twins should not be left too long playing on their own, for, like all of us, tempers can get frayed when they become bored. If the biting is aimed at preventing the twin from sharing a toy, the toy should be removed. It's impossible to know who grabbed it first.

Attention at the right times is a very good antidote for all unwanted behaviour.

The one-warning system

Three and four-year-olds are not as easily distractable as young toddlers and a one-warning system can work wonders. An example of one warning might be, 'If you don't stop banging the car on the table I shall have to take it away.' This gives the child the opportunity of stopping, rather than having the car seized before he has had a chance to do as the parents ask. If he stops banging the car he is praised for having stopped; if he continues the car is taken away without any further chances and no negative attention. More than one chance and the child won't take the parents seriously, no chances and he has no opportunity of learning self-control, of being a 'good' boy. The element of surprise may also make him react badly.

The trick is that the parents' response is immediate. If the child is told, 'If you don't stop banging the car on the table there will be no television tonight,' he is likely to ignore the threat as being too far in the future. By the time the evening has come he will probably have forgotten what it is he's supposed to have done wrong. Let's take another example: Twins are squabbling in front of the television set. The parents warn the children that if they don't stop the set will be switched off. If the children continue to squabble they will understand why the television is switched off. If they stop squabbling they are praised.

Children may get upset when parents first apply the one-warning system if they have always had several chances. However it is a great help when there are twins in the family, and they will soon learn what is and what is not permitted if parents are consistent.

Using the original example: If a child is told not to bang the car on the table one day but is allowed to do so on the next he will bang it all the more because he thinks his parents will change their mind.

The aim of the one-warning system is to stop the build up of negative attention that occurs when parents ask their children several times to do, or not to do, something without any effect. Asking can become shouting, and shouting often leads to lost tempers. Surprisingly children seem to like the one-warning system once they've got used to it. They know where they are.

Children need a few basic rules which always apply, but not so many that they feel boxed in and have to ask their parents' permission before they can do anything.

Favourites

When a mother's early preference for one twin has remained, she may find that she is trying to compensate the less-preferred twin by giving into him rather more often than to the other twin. Unfortunately, instead of making the child more lovable because he's so pleased to be favoured in this way, he discovers that his mother is a 'soft touch'! The worse he behaves, the more likely she is to give in because she feels angry with him and guilty at the same time. She negatively rewards him in two ways for his bad behaviour. She gets annoyed with him and emotionally upset, and, if he continues his bad behaviour, she gives him what he wants. This strengthens the mother's opinion that he is not a likeable child, and round the circle goes. However, the magic scissors are at hand: Stop feeling guilty!

Favourites occur in the best regulated families. Parents of several single children may say 'I love them all, but so-and-so is my favourite,' but to parents of twins it sounds terrible. It isn't. It's natural, and it often happens. Once the guilt is out of the way, the mother can stop giving in to the child whilst offering the minimum of negative attention and the maximum of positive attention for 'good' behaviour. The child finds that 'bad' behaviour does not get him what he wants and, miracle of miracles, he becomes nicer and more lovable. He may still have his moments, but they are fewer and farther between.

Some twins, particularly non-identical twins, may have a habit of telling parents about the other twin's misbehaviour. It can be difficult not to react when told, 'David's filling the basin up with water.' However, this could be a joint effort at getting attention although each twin has a different role. It is wisest not to punish the culprit, but simply quietly to deal with the situation, i.e. clear up the mess, or remove the child from possible danger. Remember that toddlers left too long on their own frequently get into mischief, and not only toddlers. By giving the minimum of negative attention parents avoid the good-twin, bad-twin labels. Special times for each twin, if at all possible, will also help to reduce the need for this kind of attention.

Choices

If a toddler is asked, 'Would you like to put your coat on?' he may not know the answer! Toddlers' motto: When in doubt, say no. His parents may then try to give him some good reasons for saying 'yes', but he's getting to enjoy the attention and says 'no' again. The parents now have three choices themselves. They can offer some more good reasons for saying 'yes', they can push the struggling child into his coat, or they can back down and say, 'Never mind, you can put it on later.' Whatever the parents do the child now thinks that they are not very sure about the whole thing. When parents are faced with a pair of twins saying 'no' the effect is doubled. The parents may wonder if the twins are right and they're making too great a fuss, or the effort of making two small people change their mind seems too much. This confirms the twins in thinking that a joint stand is the most successful one.

It's a pity really. The parents were just being polite, but 'Come and put your coat on' or 'Let's put your coat on' are less likely to confuse a small child.

A child who thinks that his parents are unable to make decisions will feel that he has to make them himself. This can be quite frightening. He'll try his best to make *all* the decisions, and when 'he' is 'they', parents can feel helpless. A change of method will be a relief to all concerned, though the children may not be quite sure at first that the parents really mean business and become more determined. This is the storm before the calm!

Twins who have confidence in their parents' decision-making will be left free to work on the business of learning and developing and in turn will learn to make their own decisions with confidence. Parents can help them to do this by offering them a choice between two alternatives: the pink dress or the blue one, for example, if either choice is acceptable to the parents.

Learning to share and work together are valuable pluses for twins who often demonstrate that two heads are better than one. However they also need to be encouraged to make individual choices, rather than by committee or by one twin being Decision-Maker-in-Chief. One way to do this is by offering two simple puzzles or learning toys, one for each twin, rather than one between two.

It may be found that there is a small difference in the twins' ability, particularly in the early stages of the children's development. Their confidence will increase if they are not over-shadowed by the co-twin and can have their own small achievements.

Time spent individually with each twin can also be used to offer choices. Quite small ones like choosing which shaped biscuit to eat, or which story they would like to be told, will help them to build up an individual identity and ability to make decisions on their own.

Bedtime problems

Toddler twins have a habit, often observed, of going berserk just before bedtime. They may do this either just before or just after they have been told that it is time for bed. It usually involves racing around the house – or one floor – at top speed, laughing, shouting, and generally working themselves up into a frenzy of excitement. This serves two purposes. It makes it almost impossible to catch both of them and they wake themselves up so thoroughly that they can't settle when finally caught and put to bed. Being chased by the parents just adds to the fun and it can turn into the most marvellous game. Some parents enjoy it, particularly the young energetic ones, and it can turn into a happy romp for all the family. However other parents run out of energy at the end of the day and would dearly love to shorten the game.

Catching twins can be quicker if both parents are available at

bedtimes, or if there is a responsible older child who can give a hand. Parents who are on their own have to persuade the twins to come to them. One method is to sound as if they're doing something much more interesting than the twins are doing. This can work at any time and is a form of distraction. At bedtimes parents can run the bath and have a very noisy, exciting time with the floating toys. If the twins are not having a bath, parents can pick a favourite book and start reading themselves a loud story or having a conversation with a glove puppet. Parents will know their own children best and what will attract their interest. The twins may stop long enough to put their heads round the door, but if parents stop what they are doing at this stage the children will probably run off again, hoping that the parents will give chase. Once children have become interested in what the parents are doing they can usually be persuaded into being put to bed or into the bath, as long as they are rewarded by the parents continuing the game or story for a little while and they are praised for coming to bed or to have their bath. They should gradually learn that the parents' game is more fun than their own.

The game of chase me doesn't only happen at bedtimes. Twins may run off just before it's time to take an older child to school or one of the twins to playgroup, or on any occasion where there is a shortage of time and, usually, a shortage of hands. The same remedy can be used, with plenty of praise when the twins join the adults.

Twins can learn that there are chase-me and not-chase-me times by being encouraged to play the game with the parents when time can be allowed for it in the garden or park. Stopping the game can be more difficult than starting it, but it can be easier if it only lasts a short time and then another game is started such as a nursery rhyme with actions, a dance, a ball game etc.

Many twins love bedtimes, but some may refuse to go to bed, particularly if an older child stays downstairs. When both refuse, parents may feel helpless, but the reward for going up without a fuss can be a bedtime story, perhaps read by the other parent. If children are close in age, another way round the problem can be for all the children to get washed and undressed at the same time, but for the older child to be allowed down again for half an hour on his own.

A good method of getting young children to behave at bedtime, is to promise bubbles in the bath if they undress themselves, or allow themselves to be undressed, quickly. It can cut short the chase-me game and stop the fuss at bedtime. As always, one-warning, and no bubbles if the behaviour doesn't stop.

Some children go to bed like lambs, but once there they keep calling out and trying to get their parents' attention. 'I'm thirsty. Can I have a drink of water?' 'I need to go to the toilet,' 'I can't sleep,' are typical cries of children from eighteen months upwards.

If parents are firm right from the start, there will be fewer problems later. If, after the first time, parents make it clear that the children must settle down and that there are to be no more requests, they should soon get the message. However, if children have not been well and have become used to broken sleep and extra attention from parents, they may continue the habit after they are better and it may take a few days before they relearn good habits.

Sometimes one twin may discover that he has found a way of getting special attention and parents may give in to him to avoid waking up the other twin, particularly if they share a room. Parents may pick a child up the minute he starts crying and toddlers can soon learn that crying brings their parents running.

It has been found that if a child wakes and is fretful and parents check that all is well but give him the minimum of attention required to settle him, this will help the child to learn good sleeping habits. Carrying the child downstairs to play, taking him into the parents' bed, or lying down with him in his own bed until he's asleep may all be difficult habits to break later. Parents taking it in turns to check the child without any fuss or undue attention will reassure the child, whilst giving him the message that he is expected to go back to sleep.

If the second twin wakes, he should be given the same minimum attention. It may mean a few disturbed nights, and perhaps the neighbours should be warned, but after a week or two, the children should decide that waking up isn't getting them special attention so they might as well go back to sleep. The advantage in having two toddlers awake is that they will sometimes give each other sufficient attention not to need any more from their parents.

Babies are not the same as toddlers and some have their wide-awake time in the middle of the night, and no amount of settling will persuade them to sleep. The health visitor is the best source of advice in these situations.

Once the children are old enough to understand, usually from about the age of three, a reward system can make all the difference when trying to develop good sleeping habits. For example, twins who have settled down quickly, stayed in bed all night, or have not called out for their parents, can be rewarded the next morning at breakfast by being given their favourite cereal or piece of fruit or whatever is a special treat for each child. The treat might be an early-morning story, but, whatever it is, it must be given as soon as possible after the children have woken up, to the accompaniment of plenty of praise. Praise is one of the best rewards that children of any age can have for being good. In this way they get their parents' attention for the right behaviour rather than for the disruptive behaviour.

Night-time waking can sometimes be due to insecurity if children feel that they have to make decisions and are not sure if their parents are in control. If parents regain control, the problem often disappears without any further action.

Bedtimes are possibly the most important rule that parents make on behalf of their children and work much better if parents are in agreement. Children who get enough sleep are usually happier in the daytime. Children who need a rest during the day often sleep better at night if they can have their rest in the morning. Parents whose children go to bed at a reasonable hour gain some well-earned space for themselves and valuable time to talk, or just be with each other.

If bedtimes are not up for discussion at the toddler stage, it will be easier when children are bigger. Parents who wait until twins are older before they take a firm line find that five-year-olds do not tuck as easily under each arm!

Misbehaving outside the home

Rather than provoke a tantrum, parents may feel that it's easier to give in to the children than have an embarrassing scene when visiting friends or relations.

Children soon find out when a different set of rules apply and are likely to take advantage of the situation, with the result that the parents' circle of friends begins to shrink.

There are few children that can handle long neighbourly chats. Most children will soon become bored and ask for drinks, biscuits, cuddles or cry that it's time to go home. This is when negative attention-seeking often begins. Long telephone conversations have much the same effect and, unless parents of twins have nerves of steel, are best left until the children have gone to bed or are being looked after by someone else.

Children can often play happily if offered small pieces of attention when parents are talking to other adults. Many parents become experts at concentrating on two conversations at once, particularly parents of twins. As children get older they will begin to play for longer periods on their own.

If the children's patience is not tried too far and parents stick to the same rules when visiting as they would at home, they should remain manageable. Antisocial twins create more havoc than a single child, but well-behaved twins are twice as impressive. Children thrive best on routine and behave better when they know what to expect.

This sounds fine, but what do parents do if they are trying to cope single-handed with the shopping and two or more under-fives and one decides to have a tantrum?

First, most small children do not like long shopping expeditions. It may be better to go for two or three short trips than one long one. Another possibility is for both parents to do the main supermarket shopping together, perhaps after work in the evening. However neither of these suggestions will necessarily prevent the problem from occurring.

One of the best ways of achieving trouble-free shopping is the Reward System. It works like this: If the children behave they are each rewarded after the checkout with a tube of Smarties or a health food bar, whatever is approved by parent and child. Any child that seriously plays up is not rewarded. It is usually best for children to be in the car or pushchair when the rewards are given, so that if one child doesn't get his, parents can remain firm. Older children can wait until they get home for the reward or until all the shopping is completed.

The same system can be used for children who play up on the way home from playgroup or nursery school.

It's important that children should see obtaining the reward in a positive way, i.e. 'If you don't have a tantrum and don't take the sweets off the shelves, you will receive the reward,' rather than, 'If you have a tantrum or grab the sweets, you will not receive the reward.' Children need to be quite clear about what they have to do to earn the reward and it should not be made too difficult. They can be reminded again if they start to misbehave and, if they then stop, the reward is still given.

A star chart is another reward system that can be very successful with older children, and some four-year-olds also respond well to it. The use of this system will be explained in Part Three, on five to twelve-year-olds.

If parents are at all worried they should consult their doctor or health visitor.

I'm having difficulty in toilet training my two-and-a-half-year-old twins. I'm quite sure that they are deliberately doing it in their nappies before I can put them on the potty. I've tried smacking them, but nothing seems to work.

You're probably right. Parents can get very uptight about toilet training and give enormous amounts of negative attention when a child doesn't oblige. The best remedy, as mentioned in this chapter, is totally to ignore failure and give a great deal of attention for success.

If the weather is mild and the house warm, there is a method that has given some very good results. Remove all garments from the waist down and place at least two potties where the children can easily find them. Removing pants and trousers makes it easy for children to use the potty or toilet without asking for help, so they don't have to wait and can be independent. Water trickling down the legs is much less comfortable than soggy clothes or a nappy which tend to retain body heat. Of course there will be plenty of accidents at first and, if at all possible, carpets and rugs should be rolled back and unwashable chairs covered or removed. Each time you see one of the twins doing it where he shouldn't, quickly put him on the pot to show him what should happen. No cross words, only praise at the first sign of success.

If there has been a new addition to the family, twins, like other children, can forget their toilet training, and it's often better to wait a few months until they have got used to the new arrival. New babies and toilet training don't mix.

I can't leave the twins together because one twin attacks the other one so violently that I am frightened of what he will do to him. How can I stop him?

Absolutely no negative attention. Each time he attacks his twin remove him to his room without saying anything and remain completely calm. Only a few minutes in his room are needed on each occasion. It's possible that he gets bored very quickly, so it may be better not to leave them playing on their own together for too long. Alternate days at playgroup, if the twins are old enough, will enable him to have some special times with you on his own without always being in competition with his twin. Treat each child as a separate individual as much as possible. This will help them both to have a sense of personal importance and identity.

Our three-year-old twins will not sit down at the table to eat their evening meal, but keep getting up and running round the room.

Perhaps the children are sitting on their own? They often behave better when an adult is sitting with them, a child on each side, even if the adult only has a cup of tea. If no one else has to sit at the table, they may not see why they should.

Tiredness can spoil the appetites of small children. They may benefit from having a slightly earlier evening meal or from having their main meal in the middle of the day. This leaves parents and any older children to have theirs in peace after the twins have gone to bed.

A reward system often works well at mealtimes, tell the twins that if they don't get down during the meal they will get a special sweet (or savoury, some children don't like sweet things) at the end of the meal. Our grandparents always believed in puddings as a treat for eating up whatever came first and, perhaps because of the emphasis on healthy eating, we sometimes forget to include them. A pudding doesn't have to be baked jam roly-poly! Jelly, yoghurt, wholefood biscuits are all very acceptable, but the rest of the family should have a sweet as well, even if it's only a piece of fruit. If the twins get down they should get one warning that they will not have their special sweet.

Don't allow the twins to take food away from the table, and, if they refuse to sit down, clear away their plates with everyone else's at the end of the meal. No negative attention, no bedtime snacks. They will make up the missing meal at breakfast and lunchtime the next day.

Small children find it difficult to sit still for very long, so it's best to leave some of the family chatter until after the meal at this stage. Praise the twins for being grown up and sitting at the table during the meal and give lots of positive attention.

Twins are not usually fussy, possibly because they know that if they don't eat up their food, there is someone else who might! If they have not had anything to eat just before the meal that could spoil their appetites, they should quickly learn not to get down during the meal.

What do I do when my twins run off in two different directions when we're out shopping or going for a walk?

If you're desperate, use reins. It's better to be safe than sorry! However, they can learn to each hold your hand or the back of the pushchair, whichever is convenient, if they are not given any choice in the matter.

What do we do when the twins keep coming out of their bedroom during 'time out'?

Ask each of them individually if they are going to be good and if they say 'yes' then they can come out. If they then repeat the behaviour, they are returned to their room. The idea is to give everyone space and a cooling-off period, not that they should remain in their room for a set period of time.

Shouldn't children have their questions answered? How are they to learn if they don't have things explained to them?

Twins tend to ask fewer questions and therefore it's very important to answer them when they ask the parent what he's doing or why things happen. Arguments should be avoided, particularly if their aim is to enable the child or children to avoid doing as you have asked.

My twins chatter away to each other, but tend to use sign language when they want something from me. I always know what it is they mean, but I'm worried that they are not really talking properly yet.

Because you understand your children so well, you are saving them the effort of explaining to you in words what it is they want.

Start by making 'please' and 'thank you' the magic words for doing as they ask. They will soon get the message if you are quite firm, but praise them when they're successful. Being consistent is very important; they have to say 'please' every time, not just sometimes. Once they have learned to say 'please' and 'thank you', the next step is for them to say the word for what it is they want. For example 'drink please', or 'garden please' if they want you to open the door for them to go into the garden. Make sure that each twin has asked you, not just one, and, again, praise for success even if they can't say the words very well at first.

Time spent with each twin on his own can be used for conversation, but make sure that *you* are talking to *them*. Alternate days at playgroup, if they are old enough, will also help them to develop their language skills. Ask your health visitor or doctor whether they feel that your twins need to be assessed by a speech therapist.

When I take the children to visit their grandparents they allow them to do things that I would not allow at home and I don't know how to persuade them to stick to our rules. What should I do?

When you are with your children, stick to your guns and keep up the consistency, but allow the grandparents to spoil them a bit when you're not around. It's a very special relationship and each child will benefit from having his grandparents to himself sometimes. By setting the grandparents an example, they will be able to see that your method works and they may well try it out for themselves when you are not there.

One of our twins creeps downstairs in the evening and we often don't realize he's in the room at first because of the noise of the television.

A gate *at the bottom* of the stairs can act as an early-warning system. It won't keep him out, but he will make a noise climbing over it. He's probably trying to get some extra attention. Be firm, take it in turns to return him to his bed, and make sure that he's having some time with you on his own, at bedtime perhaps.

My four-year-old twins get out of bed and go downstairs in the early morning. Not only do they play havoc with the kitchen, but I'm frightened they may do themselves some harm.

This time use the gate across their door. Not fixed permanently, but sufficiently firmly that they have to climb over it. This will, hopefully, wake you so that you can return them to their room. Using a play clock, show them at what time they are allowed out of bed and keep a real clock in their room if they can be trusted with it. Finally use something special at breakfast time as a reward for staying in their room until you come in for them or they are allowed to come into your room. The earlier the better, as, if they are early risers, they can get up to mischief even if they are in their own bedroom.

3
Five to Twelve

7
Family Relationships

We have looked at the way that twins under five affect the family, but as they grow older their personalities develop and relationships change.

The position that twins occupy in the family is quite important, but different from that of single children. This is because the birth order of the twins themselves may offer them another choice of position, and also because their place in the family is shared with someone else.

A middle child in a family with three children may believe that no one understands how he feels and that the other two children seem to have a more important place in the family than himself. Middle twins, on the other hand, have someone else who understands how they feel and their twinness may give them a special sense of importance.

For triplets it will be a little different. If one triplet is treated as though he is more dependable and responsible than the others, the first-born perhaps, and another triplet is treated as though he is the baby of the family, then the third triplet may not know what is expected of him or in what way he's important. This can result in negative attention-seeking which may be similar to that of some middle children. The answer is to find positive ways of showing him that he's special and not to respond to bids for negative attention. See the 'Parenting' chapter in this section.

Like a single child, the sex of a twin will affect his relationship with his parents and other children in the family, but not in quite the same way. For example, identical twin boys may have a closer relationship with father than non-identical boys. Both of these twin types may differ in turn from single boys in their relationship with father.

We have already seen that the relationship between mothers and infant twins may be affected by birth weight, but as they grow older we find that there may be a lasting effect on that relationship. Birth weight also seems to affect the way that fathers relate to their twins. For example, the lighter twin might be closer to mother, but not as close to father as his heavier brother.

Twins may pattern their own relationship on that of the parents, one often being the dominant one in the partnership. However roles may be changed, and so may dominance, during childhood.

The twin group

Within a family group there are two main sub-groups, or smaller groups: the parents' group and the children's group. When there are twins in the family there is an extra sub-group: the twin group.

Children can become disturbed because of changes within the family, but twins, particularly identical twins, may withdraw into their own little group. They then feel safer and can protect themselves, giving each other the support that they need.

The twin group can have quite a strong effect on the rest of the family. Twins may support each other in the face of opposition from the others. They may also place pressure on members of the family to join their group. Being outside a twin group can create a feeling of loneliness. If the parent group is strong enough, this can act as a counterbalance, but there are many situations where one parent may be absent either permanently or temporarily.

Sometimes one or both parents may succeed in splitting the twin group by forming an alliance with one twin. This is more likely to happen when twins are non-identical, but it can happen with identical twins as well. There may be one set of rules for one twin, another for the other. There may sometimes appear to be quite good reasons for the alliance, but it places a great deal of pressure on both twins. Parent alliances are best! Older children may also attempt to break up the twin group by making an alliance with one twin and the twins' friends may sometimes do the same. Twins having their own friends is to be encouraged, but friends who try deliberately to set one twin against the other are not very helpful.

If parents become part of the twin group, their influence can be weakened. Group support for group rules may lead parents to have self-doubts and this can affect their ability to parent, whether inside or outside the group. A parent who accepts the group's rules can also lose his own identity as an adult. If he joins the group as

leader, he may be allowed some authority, but only if the twins feel that it's in their interest!

One parent joining the twin group can also cause the other parent to feel isolated. He can then choose to join as well, or may be deliberately excluded. This parent is often the father. An isolated father means an isolated mother. She can never be a full-time member of the twin group and can become depressed because she feels that she has to cope with the children on her own.

Unlike the mother of singles, who can often lighten the burden by sharing their problems with friends in similar situations, the mother of twins may feel that no one else can really understand her difficulties.

Society tends to look on twin families as somehow special. Friends and strangers tell them how lucky they are, and there can be a feeling of letting the side down if problems are admitted. However this is where twin clubs can offer tremendous support.

Fathers may also feel overwhelmed by twins and retreat into situations where they feel they can cope. It's very important that parents make time for each other to build up their own relationship and reduce feelings of isolation. If they can also share tasks according to time and skills available and appreciate each other's efforts, both parents will grow in confidence and enjoy their twins and each other.

We have seen that there may be pressure from the twin group for a leader rather than a parent, and it can be a pressure that is difficult to resist. Because mothers are constantly dealing with a group, they may adopt a rather stronger way of dealing with their children, using anger or withdrawal of affection, rather than the 'how could you let me down?' approach. Both have their place in parenting.

Twins need a lot of organizing. Mothers as well as their children may be given the star treatment. As a result a mother of twins, even one who previously may have been shy and retiring, can find herself ready to pick up a challenge and see it through. In other words there are two sides of the coin: the self-doubts produced by a family containing a twin group, and the confidence gained by being in charge of such a group.

Most parents find that twins in the family keep them on their toes and provide a challenge that is always changing and that can be very rewarding.

Identical twins

All identical twins originate from one single fertilized cell, so they begin life with an identical blueprint. However, on the long journey from embryo to adult human being, there will be many influences that will bring about small changes.

The timing of the splitting of the cell and the way in which it splits will affect the development within the womb. One very clear effect of a different experience in the womb is that the babies often arrive with a slightly different birth weight. Being born will also be a different experience for each twin. The second twin may not have to work as hard to be born as the first, or may have a more difficult time. One twin may need extra oxygen, the other may not.

Birth order also appears to influence the personality of the identical twin. For example, first-born identical twins tend to be more independent, but, as might be expected, the personalities of both twins are very similar.

We have already seen that parents are able to pick out early differences in personality and these small differences will influence the way in which identical twins give themselves different tasks. One twin may tend to talk for both of them, or take the lead in joint enterprises. Most parents find that identical twins will often exchange roles. Like sitting on a seesaw, sometimes one is in the 'up' position, sometimes the other. However, there will be aspects of each twin's personality that will remain the same throughout childhood. As they interact with family and friends, these are reinforced and more permanent roles are established.

Identical twins seem to respond well to older children in the family, but the arrival of a younger child can affect their relationship with mother. They may become more aware of the individual attention that they have missed and resent the loss of her time and attention.

Mothers tend to be more protective of their identical twins. As infants they are sometimes more vulnerable, and identical boys can take a little longer to become socially mature. Identical twins are, by their very nature, confusing and mothers may feel that they have to try harder in order to establish a relationship.

Identical boys

Of all boys, twins or singles, identical boys tend to have the easiest relationship with their fathers. There seems to be a lack of competitiveness so often apparent between fathers and sons. This close relationship may be increased by a new addition to the family. Fathers are generally more even-handed with identical boys than mothers, but they may have difficulty in saying No and meaning it. This can result in battles which can leave everyone feeling that they have let each other down.

Mothers can be quite protective of their twin boys, particularly if one, or both, were frail at birth. They may seem to need a lot of mothering, quite apart from being exhausting. There can be a feeling that it is impossible to give them all the love and care they need.

Mothers may have different expectations of the twins according to birth order or birth weight, and be more aware of differences in personality than fathers.

Identical twin boys may take longer to lose toddler habits and this can make looking after them hard work. The close relationship between father and sons can ease the load, but can sometimes make mothers feel as if they are outside the all-male group.

It is important for mothers not to fall into the trap of feeling left out. A strong parent group can help to lessen this feeling. Time for parents to be together after the children have gone to bed and opportunities to go out regularly on their own, even if it's only for a walk or a drink at the local, can increase parent solidarity and reinforce a relationship that will, hopefully, still be there after the children have grown up.

When there is an older brother or sister, this can sometimes alter the balance in the twins' relationship with mother. This may be because the older child has not adapted very easily to the arrival of the twins and has become the family specialist in negative attention-seeking. The twins are then left with the 'good' bits. Other older children may act as an extra parent, easing the mother's load so that she has a more relaxed attitude to the twins. Identical boys generally have a good relationship with the older child.

The relationship between identical twin boys is not always a smooth one, though it can last a lifetime and mean a great deal to them. They often think and act as a pair and feel that their twin is prepared to give them more time than other members of the family and will listen to what they have to say.

Like all identical twins, their personalities will have many similarities, though different qualities will be highlighted in each twin. They are often full of energy and may prefer to be outdoors playing with their friends to occupying themselves quietly indoors.

Identical girls

Identical girls are rather like child film stars: they become used to attention and interest from an early age and, like most little girls, quite enjoy the limelight. They often make being a twin work for them and usually have an easy relationship with both adults and other children.

Identical girls tend to get on well with both parents, but one may have a special relationship with mother, the other with father. It is surprising how many parents can see a likeness to themselves in one twin, although identical twins share the same genes. Both parents tend to treat them very much alike.

The strength of this little group can sometimes be quite difficult to deal with, and mothers may use rather more emotional blackmail with their daughters than with their sons.

Identical girls tend to be critical of older brothers or sisters, particularly brothers, who may be having a hard time coping with two starlets in the family. The older child may deal with this by distancing himself from the family. If there is a close relationship between the mother and the older child, the twins may move closer to father.

Identical girls tend to be a fairly close twosome, often being each other's best friend. They may feel that their twin is the only one who really understands them and personal problems are often sorted out within the twin group. This can make them easy family members, often with an easy relationship between themselves.

However, the 'close twosome' can sometimes be too close for comfort and lead to arguments and feelings of resentment. One member of an identical pair, now grown up, remembers the mixed feelings she had about her twin and how she suffered because of the constant remarks and comparisons by others. She was made to feel somehow guilty for being slightly taller than her twin. One day she asked her mother why she could not have a bicycle like her friend Joan. She was told that she should consider herself lucky because she had a twin sister and Joan did not. At the time, she remembers, she would have gladly exchanged her twin for a bicycle. However she was deeply hurt when her twin decided to assert her independence by moving out of their shared bedroom.

Like identical boys, the girls' relationship with each other may go through changes, but as they grow older patterns tend to become set. Their relationship can vary from being very close knit, to both having separate interests and separate friends as well as those in common.

Non-identical twins

Non-identical twins commonly share anything between forty and sixty per cent of their genes, unlike identical twins who have the same genetic blueprint. They will be as alike, or as unalike, as any two children in the same family. In spite of this, non-identical twins often think that they are more alike because they are twins and there is a sense in which they are right.

The non-identical twin's experience of life is shaped, not only by his own personality and the family into which he's born, but also by being born a twin and having a twin as a companion. Unlike other children he has shared his mother both in the womb and after with a brother or a sister at the same stage of development as himself.

This affects his relationships within the family in a unique way and makes him not only similar in some ways to his twin brother or sister, for example in language development and the way he expresses himself, but also to other non-identical twins. The non-identical twin has to have his twinness taken into consideration just as much as the identical twin.

Although birth weight differences seem to have an effect on family relationships, birth order differences appear to be important as well. This may be because it is stressed by the parents. There are some indications that if there is an older child in the family they will see birth order as important and communicate this to the twins. Twins themselves may see it as a way of asserting their differences. Identical twins, too, may see birth order in this light. There may also be prenatal reasons for birth order differences.

There is a greater likelihood that the first-born in a pair of non-identical twins will become the leader of the pair, whilst the second-born may, like many younger children, be rather more light-hearted and quicker to see the funny side of things. The second-born may also have a little more difficulty in accepting a new addition into the family.

Birth order has little effect on mixed-sex twins because being a boy or girl is more important. In other words, being a mixed-sex twin is a different experience from being a same-sex non-identical twin. This is different in turn from being an identical twin.

Many researchers have tested twins to find out how similar they are in personality and IQ. The most surprising finding is that mixed-sex twins are often more alike than same-sex non-identicals. One reason may be that whilst same-sex twins tend to stress their differences as well as their similarities, and compete with each other, there is less need for mixed-sex twins to do so. The differences between them are obvious to everyone and they are perhaps in a special position to learn from each other. For example, the boy may be a little more gentle, the girl rather more assertive.

Non-identical same-sex: boys

Fathers are generally firmer with these twins than with identical boys and, though aware of personality differences, tend to treat them in much the same way. Mothers are more likely to have a different style of parenting for each twin, but be close to both boys. These boys can sometimes lack confidence and the close relationship with mother can have its ups and downs. It may also leave father feeling that he is outside the group and perhaps in competition with the boys for the mother's time and attention.

It's important for twins to know that there are occasions when their mother and father want to do things together and that they have to take second place.

All parents are much more aware of personality differences between non-identical twins, but mothers tend to respond to these differences rather more. This can affect relationships throughout the family. She may respond to birth order differences, but birth weight differences seem to have a greater effect on non-identical boys and the way that they relate to both parents.

Non-identical boys tend to be home-loving and may need encouragement to tackle new tasks. Their twin relationship may not be as important as that of identical boys, but constant companionship can sometimes forge strong links. Their twin is less of a threat to their own identity than in the case of identical boys.

Non-identical same-sex: girls

Most girl twins have an easier relationship with their father than single daughters, but these girls can be quite a powerful duo, exerting a strong group pressure. Parents who have a strong group of their own can help to maintain a good balance.

Mothers tend to have a close relationship with these daughters, though it may not be roses all the way. They may find it difficult to resist joining the twin group. Mothers often have a different style of parenting for each twin, whilst fathers tend to be more even-handed.

Relationships with other children in the family can be mixed and may differ from one twin to the other. Outside the home they may make the most of being twins.

Non-identical girls often become each other's best friend and can have a close relationship, similar in many ways to that of identical girls. However they are more likely to compete with each other and less likely to swap jobs within the partnership. If they are too much in each other's company they are less likely to find out what they can do on their own without the help or hindrance of the twin.

These twins can sometimes feel that their co-twin has a duty to supply their needs for help and companionship, and this can be reinforced by parents. They may feel badly let down when the help is not forthcoming. This is where they may differ from identical girls who frequently give each other support without any outside encouragement.

Non-identical girls can feel quite irritated by their twin on occasions in spite of their close relationship, but they usually remain friends.

Mixed-sex twins

The girls of mixed-sex twins often enjoy a good relationship with their father, which is similar to that of identical girls. However they can sometimes be in competition with him which can lead to arguments. They generally have a good relationship with their mother and may be looked upon as the big sister of the boy twin. This can place them in quite a strong position in the family. They tend to mature rather faster than their brothers who can sometimes find family relationships rather more difficult.

Birth order seems to have much less influence on family relationships for these twins, but heavier birth weight sons can sometimes have a rather stronger relationship with father than lighter birth weight sons.

Although the girl is often the dominant partner in the pair, the weight, height, rate of maturity (both physically and mentally) of the boy can alter the family pattern.

Relationships with an older brother or sister can be difficult, though sometimes one twin can make an alliance with an older brother or sister of the same sex as themselves.

The relationship between the twins themselves is an interesting one, having much in common with identical twins, though some pairs tend to each go their separate ways. It seems to be a rather all-or-nothing relationship.

Girls in a mixed-sex twinship are rather similar in personality to identical girls, but boys tend to have characteristics in common with both identical and non-identical twin boys.

Older brothers and sisters

Parents often feel that they are closer to the older brother or sister than they are to the twins. This is not surprising when it is remembered that parents have had some time to get to know the older child before the twins arrived. Even after the twins' arrival, there are usually more opportunities to talk to the older child on his own.

Parents are generally sympathetic towards the older child and understand that having twin brothers or sisters cuts down on the amount of time and attention he is able to have. Parents will often make a special effort to give him more time, for example by letting him stay up after the twins have gone to bed.

The older child may resent the amount of time that his mother spends with the twins. He may be less likely to ask for a cuddle or bring his problems to her, feeling that he has to be independent. He may compensate for this by moving closer to father.

Most older brothers and sisters of twins manage to adapt, and often the shorter the age gap the easier it is for them. They may sometimes feel a little guilty about their jealous feelings and try hard to be kind to the twins and help look after them. But for some, particularly those who have had their parents to themselves for a few years, there can be difficulties. Boys seems a little more vulnerable than girls, who are more likely to enjoy being the twins' big sister and to use them as a way of getting attention for themselves. Girls are more likely to help their parents look after the twins and to see themselves as important members of the family. They are also more likely to be close to one of the twins. Boys, on the other hand, who are generally less skilled socially than girls, often feel overshadowed and pushed out.

When there are more children in the family, the older child may be better able to deal with the situation. If there is another brother or sister close in age they will often turn to each other, forming another pair within the family. If there is only one older child he may look outside the family for companionship, or may try hard to join the twin group, perhaps by becoming their leader. He will sometimes form an alliance with one twin in order to split the pair. Arguments are not uncommon!

The older child can become very conscious of his oneness if his parents are together and form a second pair – everyone seems to have a companion except himself. A younger child too can sometimes feel deprived of a playmate.

In spite of the difficulties, the older brother or sister of twins is generally more involved with his younger twins than he would have been if there had been only one younger child.

I'm at the end of my tether with my identical boys. I'm quite strict with them, but it seems to be a perpetual battle. My husband is more inclined to give in to them, but they can make even him lose his temper.

This is a very typical family pattern with identical boys.

It can be a great help for both parents if they can sit down and decide together how they are going to deal with certain pieces of behaviour. This will help to stop the boys feeling 'dad lets me do it, why can't mum?' If the boys feel that they're dealing with both of you at the same time, even when you're not actually together, they will be more likely to back down quickly without a great scene and less likely to push dad until he loses his temper.

I expect you're also fed up with always being the bad guy, so here's a way of being the good guy without having to give in to the twins: Decide with your husband on two pieces of behaviour that always provoke a scene. For example, bedtimes and clearing toys away. Make a star chart as shown on page 169, and award one star to each twin each day that there are no scenes at bedtime and the toys are cleared away without a fuss. Five stars earn a small reward like a packet of stickers, some sweets, a colouring book, whatever the children like, is cheap, and parent-approved. Every time they each reach five stars they get a small prize.

There may be different pieces of bad behaviour that you would like each twin to stop, or you may choose the same ones for both twins. Once the behaviour is changed, stars can be awarded for another piece of behaviour, cleaning teeth perhaps. The 'Parenting' chapter (page 102) gives more information on the 'star system'. You now become the nice mum and dad who hand out prizes for good behaviour. Bad behaviour receives the minimum of negative attention.

How is it that identical girls, who you say can be very easy members of the family, can become isolated and shut everyone else out?

There may be many reasons. They might have been isolated by circumstances and thrown continuously on each other's company. Parents may have lost their confidence as parents when faced with two, so that the twins became too powerful as a pair. Or parents may have been so proud of having twin girls that they over-emphasized their twinness and the twins lost their sense of individual identity. These extreme cases are unusual, but professional help at an early stage can prevent the problem becoming severe.

My wife is a wonderful mother and does everything for our non-identical boys, but sometimes I feel that she is wearing herself out. I find it difficult to convince her.

It may be that you need to help your wife to get out more. Try to arrange to leave the boys with a reliable baby-sitter and take her out at least once a month. Think of something you know she will enjoy, but not break the bank. Encourage her to follow some of her own interests and offer to look after the boys for her sometimes, even if it's only whilst she has a coffee with the next-door neighbour.

My work takes me away from home sometimes and when I come home I feel as if I'm in the way. My twin girls will often exchange looks if I say or do anything that they don't like and I feel my wife doesn't give me enough support.

The twin group can be a very difficult one to deal with if you feel you're on the outside. Find opportunities of getting to know your twins individually and try to treat them as less of a pair. Use their individual names (you may be doing so already, of course); help your wife to be firm about bedtimes so that you can have time together after the girls have gone to bed. Perhaps it might be possible to take your wife with you on one of your trips, leaving the children with grandparents or a reliable friend. A strong parent group is good for the twins and good for you.

My daughter fusses over her twin brother like an old hen. They're six and he still can't tie his own shoelaces yet; she does them for him. If another child picks on him at school, she takes the other child on. She doesn't give him a chance to do anything by himself. If we tell him off, he bursts into tears and runs to his sister.

If it's possible, place them in separate classes and then separate schools when they change to middle school. Encourage your husband to spend time with the boy on his own, so that he can learn new skills and enjoy his dad's approval. Have confidence in your son and help your daughter to have confidence in him too. Perhaps you and your daughter could have special times together as well.

My eight-year-old daughter is better at playing football than her brother and all the boys want her to come out and play with them, but they don't want my son. He's always getting headaches and stomach aches and I'm really worried about him. My husband says he should just go out and play and not wait to be asked, but I don't like to push him.

Encourage your son to join some clubs, particularly those which are for boys only, so that he can make friends without competing with his sister. He may have a gift for music or acting which you could encourage, or he may be good at gymnastics or canoeing. Look for an interest in which your daughter does not excel and let him pursue it on his own.

Different schools can make a big difference to mixed-sex twins who are being overshadowed by the co-twin. Try and find out what is available in your area. Separate classes can also help to ease the situation if the twins are not already separated.

Again, encourage your husband to spend time with him on his own and this will also give you some time with your daughter. Have confidence in your son.

My daughter simply adores her brother and just sits around the house doing nothing whenever he goes out to play with his friends. I can't persuade her to make her own friends and she can't understand that boys don't always want a girl around. Will she grow out of it, or should I insist that her brother takes her with him?

No twin should have their co-twin forced upon them and your son and his friends may be going through the anti-girl phase. It doesn't usually last very long.

This is really the previous problem in reverse and the same answer applies. Encourage your daughter to develop her own interests and gifts. Take her out sometimes by herself, or with a friend. Invite a friend to stay the night with her and help to make the evening fun. Hopefully the friend will want to stay again and your daughter will gain confidence in making friends and keeping them. Separate classes or schools would be helpful, if available.

Our older child is always helping himself to things out of the refrigerator. Also, we're not sure, but we think that there may be money missing sometimes.

This is a compliment, really. He's trying to tell you that he'd like a bit more of you than he's getting.

By stealing he's getting a lot more negative attention. Be firm without making a fuss and step up the positive attention by praising good behaviour. A star system is a very useful method and you will find out how to use this on page 113. Perhaps dad could also find some special times to be with him. If it could be on a regular day and time, your son would be able to look forward to it.

In the meantime I shouldn't leave money around. Better to avoid temptation. Make sure he has regular pocket money of his own, even if it's only a few pence.

My daughter is easily irritated by her twin sisters and there is always shouting and screaming.

Leave them to it. It may be a way of getting negative attention. If it gets too bad, be very calm and send the children to their own rooms to cool down. Don't listen to tale-bearing; it's almost impossible to know who has the right story. Do give your older daughter special privileges for being the eldest, even though you may not think that she deserves them. Don't be pressured by the twins into giving them the same. Try and have some outings, just you and your daughter, even if it's only to the shops. Children are usually much nicer on their own. It will help you to resist her negative attention-seeking at other times.

When your daughter next changes school, it might be helpful if it can be arranged for the twins not to follow her there, but to go to a different school if available.

8
The Couple Effect

This term was invented by Professor Zazzo who observed that being part of a twin group affected the twins in a variety of ways.

The first way, as we found in Part Two, is through language. Not only does it effect the rate of language development, but twins who spend their early years together may develop a private language. For others it may be a private shorthand containing words and gestures that convey instant messages to their twin. These messages, based on their joint experience of the world, serve to confirm their 'twin sided' viewpoint. Together they build up their own twin culture which may not be exactly the same as that of family and friends. This bond that is expressed in language has been called by Zazzo their 'Secret Garden' – a place where only they may enter.

The second way in which twins are affected by being a couple is in the allocation of tasks.

Whenever two people live together, they will usually decide what each one's duties are. There are the small ones, like who washes and who dries, and the bigger ones like who does the decorating, cooking, gardening, managing the accounts. Some of these may be shared, but there will usually be some division of labour within the task.

There are still many wives who find themselves alone and in difficulty because they can't mend a fuse or understand the accounts. Once they tackle the task they may find that they have skills they were unaware of. They had simply never developed them.

Tasks can be emotional as well as practical. One partner may be the one that makes friends and brings them home, the other may like reading or music. One may go to pieces in a crisis, the other get upset by small things, each complementing each other.

Because twins are a couple who usually spend all their childhood together, they may prevent each other from developing certain skills, practical or emotional. Each has been allocated his duties from an early age. The more closely coupled their lives have been, the more likely they are to specialize. They become like two pieces of a jigsaw puzzle, each needing the other to make him complete. One may do the talking, the other remain silent or chime in at the end of sentences. They may share the sentences, rather like partners in a tennis game, requiring both members to keep a conversation going. One twin may lead, the other follow like a shadow, letting the first twin test out the ground. If the balance in the relationship alters, tasks may be reallocated.

Although such twins may appear to be very different in personality, they may be closer than twins who are more similar. Twins who have been separated in early childhood are often more alike than those brought up together. They have been able to develop all their skills free from the couple effect.

The Couple Effect is also influenced by the twin type. For example, identical twins in competition may deliberately hold back and pace themselves on each other, whilst non-identical twins in the same situation will often try harder.

Finally, because twins are a couple they tend to act as a group. They reinforce each other's opinions and they may become more rigid and less open to persuasion. This can make non-identical twins more alike. However, they may also find it more difficult to make independent decisions and have a weaker sense of identity, particularly identical twins.

The Couple Effect, with its division of tasks between twins, is possibly the greatest cause of worry for parents and teachers. However, if twins are treated as two separate individuals and encouraged to have their own friends and interests as well as shared ones, they will learn to develop the skills that are needed when their twin is not available. Though there may still be some specialization, it will be within acceptable limits and they will not be tied permanently together.

9
Education

Starting school

The 'plus' in 'five-plus' probably stands for 'at last I've got a bit of time to myself!'

Twins are expensive, no hand-me-downs and two of everything, so mothers may now start to look for a part-time job if they have not already found one. Not only does this help the household budget but it also offers the opportunity to spend some time with adults to whom they are not 'the twins' mother'. It's unlikely that colleagues will be left in ignorance for long!

If there are no younger children, the absence of the twins can feel very strange at first. Parents who have been waiting longingly for the first day of school may find themselves waiting equally anxiously for school to finish at the end of the day.

When a child begins school there are always mixed feelings, but when two children go together the loss is even greater. A wise mother prepares herself, if she is not returning to work, by becoming involved in outside activities well before school starts. She then has something of her own to look forward to during the week.

Children who sense that their mother is unhappy when they leave for school may find all sorts of excuses to stay at home with her and can become distressed themselves.

Many mothers look forward to having the day to themselves, others manage to look convincingly cheerful even if they don't feel it. For those who find it difficult, it can sometimes be helpful if father, or another mother, can take the children to school. Collecting the children from school is no problem.

The pain of loss gradually disappears as mothers find the time that the twins are at school goes all too quickly. However at the start of each term the home will feel strangely quiet.

If there is any child who persistently finds it difficult to go to school, professional help should be obtained.

School can bring a different set of problems. The twins will be in the spotlight and differences will be observed and possibly exaggerated. One twin may make friends more easily than the other. Just as problems at home can be carried over into the classroom, so can classroom problems affect the twins' behaviour at home.

Both twins will want to tell the parent about their day and time should be given to each, without too much interruption from the other, to have their say. The first ten minutes at home are always important for any age group. A drink, a snack, a sympathetic ear, and small worries are less likely to become big ones.

Twins who have been used to some independence at school will cope better when they have to go on their own if one of the pair is unwell. However, being at home on their own can be particularly rewarding for twins for whom a whole day with the parent on his own can prove irresistible. Non-specific complaints such as a stomach ache should be watched if they occur too frequently. If symptoms fade away as soon as remaining at home for the day is assured, or only occur on certain days, then the best remedy may be to send the child to school.

Always take the child for a medical checkup, as it will serve to put the parents' minds at rest. If the child is given a clean bill of health, alert the teacher so that an eye can be kept on the child at school. It is also as well to check that there are no problems at school which might be causing anxiety.

Once the decision has been made to send the child regularly to school, the symptoms may become worse. Although very real to the child while the pain lasts, this subconscious plea for attention should be resisted. This type of behaviour can follow a previous, genuine bout of illness which has convinced the child of the pleasures of being at home.

If the pains have not decreased in frequency within a fortnight of the child being sent regularly to school, seek further professional advice.

Together or apart?

Some schools have a policy of placing twins in separate classes, others feel that whatever the relationship between twins, they should always be together. Most leave it up to the parents.

This may be the most important decision that parents make. Often otherwise trouble-free twins may have problems at school caused by unequal ability, unequal division by the twins of educational tasks, language difficulties and unequal teaching, to name but a few.

Sometimes there is no choice, particularly at first schools where there may only be a single form entry.

Children who have attended nursery school on separate days will usually adapt well to being in separate classes. Separate classes, if at all possible, will prevent many of the problems already mentioned, except for that of unequal teaching.

Parents are always anxious to give all their children, not just twins, equal opportunities. However, no two children are the same and teachers are not identical either. There may be difficulties if two class teachers are using very different teaching methods. They may both be equally good, but problems can occur if twins, or parents, believe that one is being held back. It may be wise to enquire beforehand what methods the two parallel classes are using and whether it would be possible to find some common links that will make sense to the twins. For example, if one teacher allows books to be read at home and the other teacher does not, one child may feel that he is falling behind the other. Perhaps both twins could be allowed to take their reading books home, or one twin could be allowed to take books home from the school library. If there appears to be a great deal of difference in the achievement of the two classes, it may be better to keep the twins in the same class, at least for the first year. Twins who have not been used to separation often settle into school more easily if they start in the same reception class.

Another reason for *not* separating twins is if there have been any major upheavals in the family. Moving house, the loss of a loved relation, separation or divorce of the parents will all affect the twins and they will gain comfort from remaining together.

If twins are to be kept in the same class, it's a good idea to sit them at different tables, well apart from each other. They will then be less likely to respond to the teacher and other children as a pair. They should also be encouraged to partner other children in the class rather than choosing the twin as a partner for all activities. If twins are difficult to prise apart, this can be done slowly and gently, commencing with just one activity.

If at all possible, mixed-sex twins are best placed in separate classes as socially and academically they are less likely to progress at the same rate. It is helpful for them to develop at their own pace.

Newly separated twins may need to be reassured by the occasional visit to the other twin's classroom during the day, and a place kept next to their twin at lunchtimes. Once they have settled in they may prefer to sit next to their new friends.

Twins can often mask learning difficulties in the co-twin by doing the work for them or showing them how to do it. They may decide to specialize. If one learns to read, for example, before the other, the co-twin may decide that this is not his job. Like one identical twin who told his mother, 'I don't see why I need to read if David can.' Sometimes one twin can be so de-skilled that he can become over-anxious and almost allergic to certain tasks at which he feels his twin is better. Separation and gentle encouragement can usually help him to overcome the difficulty.

Twins are used to working together and are likely to do so at home as well as at school. A deficiency in one may go unnoticed for several years. If, having been together, they are then split up, perhaps for social reasons, this can be a difficult experience for the less able twin. He may find himself unable to keep up with the other children in the class. An early diagnosis of his problem, gentle encouragement, and perhaps some extra coaching will help to restore his confidence.

Although twins may often work together and produce a piece of homework by 'committee', it is not unusual for identical twins to produce almost identical work without conferring – in a test, for instance.

If twins are together it can be difficult for teachers to judge their individual work at any stage of their school careers, and school reports often reflect this, like an identikit picture, one being superimposed upon the other.

It can be a great help to teachers if twins are dressed differently so that they can respond to them individually. Different hairstyles, or haircuts, are particularly useful as they prevent playful twins from substituting for each other if one doesn't like a particular lesson or activity. One little girl who didn't like going to the school dentist, sent her twin sister in twice.

As we have seen, the development of language ability may be a little behind that of single children. Some twins, particularly boy twins, can take rather longer to settle down at school. Twins understand each other more easily than their classmates or teachers, and the gap may widen. Separate classes will usually help them to adapt more quickly. Most twins catch up by the time they are about eight, though some may always slightly underachieve through no fault of their own. Awareness of the need for extra help in this area, as early as possible in their school career, is important. Bright twins who are held back by poor language can become bored and difficult.

Teachers are often happy to work out a programme with parents to enable them to help their twins at home. Most children respond well to parents who take an interest in their schoolwork in a friendly and positive way and who praise achievement.

Five to ten minutes spent each evening on reading a simple book together will encourage reading ability. If the child loses confidence, parent and child could read alternate sentences. The task is then less likely to become too difficult or boring. Many parents find that they cannot be patient with their own children, and a limited time spent on reading will often prevent frayed tempers. Sometimes one parent, or an older brother or sister, has more patience with a particular child, in which case the job can be handed over to them. Games which involve language, such as Scrabble, are also helpful, and teachers can be approached to suggest others that parents can use to teach their children in a way that is fun for everyone.

Lack of verbal skills may cause twins to misunderstand questions, though they may be quite able to provide the answers once the question has been explained. A little extra time taken to make sure that each child understands what is wanted of him could save a lot of tears and frustration later. Children are often too embarrassed to ask for explanations in front of their classmates.

Twins are not the only ones to have language problems. Teachers will be familiar with single children who have similar problems, and these often come to the surface rather more quickly as twins can cover up for each other's shortcomings. Two heads are better than one!

It is important that twins are not held back because of poor written work if it is clear that they are capable of tackling the task set. They may have other skills that can be used to enable them to produce the work in a more practical form. Twins can sometimes get 'stuck' on written work, afraid that they won't be able to produce what the teacher wants. Awareness that a bright twin may not always be able to do himself justice can help the teacher to dissuade him gently from setting himself impossible standards. In time the child should learn the skills he needs if he is encouraged in such a way that he does not lose confidence.

The twins' need for attention may often show itself in the classroom. Little girls may try to attract the teacher's attention by being especially good and helpful, but they may also compete with their twin and their classmates for her time. If twin boys have been a handful at home, they may take this into the classroom. Joint strategies between parents and teachers in dealing with certain behaviours can be useful, particularly the use of a star system. In order not to draw too much attention to the twins, stars may be awarded in a notebook to be taken home at the end of each week. Parents can then award a small prize if a certain number of stars have been given by the teacher.

Comparison between twins at school needs to be avoided as much as possible. Even identical twins are not identical in every way. Separate classes are often the answer to unequal ability. Twins who are very similar in ability may still decide that one is the 'clever' one. The co-twin may carry the label 'not so clever' all his life. The same can apply to competitive games.

Constant front-runners in a set of twins may have a bad reaction if the tables are turned and their co-twin comes in first. They may have come to look on being better than their twin as their natural right, and coming second can cause them to stop trying. If they can be taught to measure themselves against their own achievements rather than those of their twin, this will help to reduce the problem. Unfortunately others may still compare them and cause difficulties. Sometimes separate schools are the only answer, if at all possible.

The educational crunch usually comes at secondary school when differences in ability and skills, if any, may finally have to be faced. Twins who may not have been separated before, may find themselves in different classes, different ability groups, or even in different schools.

Parents may have to decide whether to send both twins to an all-ability school or each to a school that suits his particular gifts; or one where classes are streamed, the other where children are in the same class but may be placed in different groups.

Parents have to make their own choices, but clearly they will be influenced by the special advantages of a particular school, such as the quality of the teaching, the subjects offered, the atmosphere of the school, nearness to home etc. This can make the decision more difficult. Do parents separate their twins, which means that both twins cannot go to the preferred school, or do they send them to the same school at the risk of the twins being compared, or comparing themselves, and one feeling at a disadvantage? Very much depends on the degree of separation possible within the preferred school and the extent to which being in the same school is causing problems. Sometimes parents are given no choice in the matter. When in doubt, professional advice may be helpful.

Remedial help may be suggested if one or both twins are having difficulties. Very occasionally it may be suggested that one of the twins repeats a year, although this is not the general practice in the U.K. It generally causes more problems than it solves. Parents and teachers should look at the child's progress in relation to the rest of the class, not just in relation to the twin. If a child is having a real struggle then another school with, perhaps, smaller classes or extra remedial teaching may help to do himself greater justice. If the decision is made that he should repeat a year then, again, it would be better to do this in a different school where comparisons will not be made. He will then not have his twin as a constant reminder of where he 'ought' to be, and the other twin will not have the guilt feelings about achieving more than his twin. It will also be easier, when he comes to school-leaving age, for him to make the decision about whether or not to stay on at school. He

will, hopefully, be more influenced by his own classmates and teachers than by what his twin may have decided to do.

Once again it should be emphasized that if there have been any major upheavals in the family, then this is not the time to separate them if they have always been together. If they have already been separated they might wish to be together for a while until things have settled.

Competitiveness between twins can sometimes cause problems at this stage. Children can overwork themselves and parents who have high fliers, or even just average twins who are trying to outdo each other, should make sure that the competition does not get out of hand. If twins can be encouraged to have separate out-of-school activities and interests, this will give them a break from schoolwork and a break from each other. If this is difficult, leisure time could become a family habit when everyone stops what they are doing for half an hour or so to go for a walk or play a game together.

A certain amount of competitiveness can be helpful and many twins have encouraged each other to do well on the sports field or academically, and have achieved more than they would have done without this incentive. For some identical twins, doing better than a previous best is the duty of both twins and it is not important which one achieves it. In other words, they are not competing separately, but together.

Language can still be a problem for older twins, even the brightest. This may appear as 'laziness' in presentation, 'muddled' thinking and 'stupid' mistakes. Teachers can help by trying to find out what the youngster is trying to say and encouraging him to find the right words in the right order. It can be very frustrating for twins who know the answers but whose written work can't keep up with their own speed of thinking. A pocket dictionary can be invaluable.

Twin boys in particular may 'play dumb' rather than look foolish in class. Instead of asking them to reply in front of the other children, it may be better to ask them questions about their work on an individual basis.

Praise

Another problem that parents and teachers often have with twins, is a worry about giving too much praise to one in case the other becomes upset. If they do praise one, they may try and restore the balance by praising the other twin as well. This can create the impression that the parent, or teacher, is never especially pleased with the particular achievement. The child then either gives up or is forever searching for a satisfaction that seems to escape him. Praise should be given when deserved and opportunities will occur to praise the other twin without artificially creating them. A good teacher praises effort, and this is a useful hint for parents of twins. Each twin is entitled to his moment of glory without having to share it. If the co-twin needs a little sympathy, this can be saved for a quiet time when the child is on his own.

There is a difference between praise that needs to be an immediate reaction to a piece of behaviour or to an announcement by the child of some special achievement, and praise that can be delayed and given when the other child is not necessarily close by. A telling-off can follow the same rule.

Twins who are in separate classes make it much easier for parents and teachers to praise achievement because it is not related to the other twin. School reports which contain a mixture of success and failure are best read with each twin on his own and should remain confidential unless the twins want to tell each other. The same applies, of course, to an older child.

Mixed-sex twins are almost always best in separate classes where their different gifts can be developed to the full without looking over their shoulders.

Triplets

A word about triplets. Triplets are sometimes made up of a pair of identical twins, plus a non-identical third child, or a pair of one sex and one of the other. Parents or teachers may be tempted to place the matching pair in one class and the odd one in another, hoping that it may be easier for the third child to be on his own. Unfortunately this is often stressful for the third child who can feel even more of an outsider in the threesome. It is usually best to keep them all together and wait to separate them until they go to a larger school which may have three parallel classes.

All three children should be placed in different groups in the classroom if this is possible, or sit between two other children.

If there is a boy with two girls in a set of triplets, and he is already being shut out or de-skilled, he may need separate schooling, preferably single sex. Again parents have to make do with what is available. Time with father is very important, as with mixed-sex twins.

It is almost impossible to separate more than three, but as the numbers increase, so do the number of possible pairings.

Older brothers and sisters

This section should not finish without a thought for the older brother or sister of twins.

If there is a very positive relationship between the older child and the twins, there may well be no problem. The older child may be proud of having 'his' twins at school and show them off to his friends, or he may lead a completely independent life.

However there are some children, particularly those who are close in age to the twins, who may feel overshadowed. Some twins report back to the parents when the older child misbehaves, so that he feels as if he's being constantly watched. Even though parents may sometimes find these reports useful, they should be discouraged, as with reports about the other twin. The older child is entitled to his privacy.

Older children may also feel envious of the attention that twins continue to get, even in school, and react badly. The older child may be known as 'the twins' brother (or sister)' a doubtful claim to fame as 'the twins' mother' may herself feel sometimes.

Older children may be desperate for attention and have difficulty in their relationships at school. The best way of helping them may be by sending them to a different school from the twins. Parents and teachers can also work on a programme of not rewarding negative attention-seeking, but rewarding positives. A star system may be very useful in this situation. Again, teachers may work with parents so that a reward can be given at home and the spotlight is not shone too brightly on the child.

The teacher might suggest professional help, and whoever is involved may well work with the school on such a system, or help the parents along these lines.

One of our non-identical twins is very upset because he's in a different class from his brother and he's on a different reading system. His brother is allowed a new book every week, whilst he has the same book for several weeks at a time. What should we do?

Have a chat with both teachers. Perhaps he could be taking other books home to read at the same time as his brother, or both twins could be on the same system. Teachers can sometimes take the attitude that it was your choice to separate them and you have to take the consequences. Don't be discouraged. Talk to both class teachers in order to reach a compromise.

My daughter refuses to write. There is a small difference in ability between the twins but it's very slight. She becomes anxious when asked to write anything and we're rather worried.

The answer could be separate classes so that she is no longer watching her sister. With gentle encouragement she should regain her confidence. Alternatively the teacher might decide to use a star system, starting with a star for writing her name, and building up until she earns a star for writing a whole sentence.

Our eight-year-old twin boys are finding it difficult to sit still in school and the teacher complains that they are disturbing the class.

Put into action the suggestions from the 'Parenting' chapter (page 102) about being firm, ignoring bad behaviour and rewarding good behaviour. Tell the teacher what you are doing so that you can both work together. This way the boys will get the message more quickly and begin to settle down.

My twin son and daughter both do athletics and games at school, and both are good, but my son wins all the prizes. My daughter says she's fed up with games. What should we do? We try not to make a fuss of him when she's around, but it doesn't seem to make any difference.

Your son needs praise and your daughter is probably quite proud of him really. Tell her that she's very kind not to want to compete with him so that he can be special, but that they don't have to be in competition. She can enjoy sport because it's fun, not to win prizes. Perhaps your daughter could be encouraged to take part in an activity, either during or after school, on her own where she does not feel in competition with her brother. Help them to appreciate each other's strong points.

Different schools can be helpful for mixed-sex twins who may be always looking over their shoulders.

One of our twins is much less clever than the other but it wasn't until they started school that it really showed. The teachers have kept them together in the same group so that the brighter twin can help the other one, but it is holding her back and not really helping her sister to stand on her own feet.

Separate classes and possibly separate schools may be the best answer. One may move ahead of the other and they will probably quite happily accept the situation if they can make their own friends at their own level. It will make it easier for you to praise them both when they do well, without any comparison with their twin.

One of our twins takes hours over her homework and becomes upset when we try to help her. She seems able to do the work, but lacks confidence. Her twin sister has no problem at all.

It looks as though she is comparing herself with her twin and separate classes might help.

Have a word with her teacher about the problem and find out if she is having any difficulties at school. Also ask the teacher how long she is meant to spend on her homework, then allow her the official time plus fifteen minutes. Some children need a little extra time.

Settle both twins down before the evening meal, with the television switched off until the time is up, even if one twin has finished before the other. If your daughter has not finished within the time, write a note to the teacher saying how long she has spent on her homework. This will help the teacher to find out where the problem lies.

Look for plenty of opportunities to praise her, including effort, and reduce the attention for getting upset. Quite difficult sometimes, I know. A star system might also be useful. One star, say, for settling down quickly to her work and another for not making a fuss (which includes asking for help without getting upset). As soon as she begins to get upset withdraw from the situation. Stars can be awarded to her sister for two quite different tasks.

One of my eleven-year-old identical twins refuses to go to school. She clings to me crying, and, if I make her go, she refuses to go into class.

Have they been placed in different classes recently or in different ability groups? If so she may have been relying on her twin for several years and now she has a lot of catching up to do. If she is of similar ability to her twin, have a chat with her teachers and see if she can have some extra coaching or some work that you could help her with at home. Explain to her that she has to go to school, but that the teachers understand her problem and will help her. Perhaps she could be encouraged to succeed in non-academic subjects until she has caught up.

It's possible that she may have no problem in doing the work but lacks confidence because her sister is not with her. Her class teacher might arrange for another child to take her under her wing for a bit until her confidence has come back. Perhaps the friend could be invited home.

If she continues to be unhappy, think about whether there have been recent changes in the family that could be making her feel insecure.

Our twins are wonderful friends to each other and love to be together. We've had no problems with their education at all. They are both a good average, do well in school and have lots of friends. We would just make them unhappy if we tried to separate them.

You obviously have a very close pair of twins and I can understand why you are worried by the idea of separating them.

I recommend that you read Part Four 'Adolescence and After', which might help you to reach a final conclusion?

If in the future you do decide to separate them, I suggest you wait until the next change of school. If this is a secondary school, then you might choose a school where they would be together for certain subjects and activities. You could have a chat with the prospective headteacher, or teachers, and see what is available and whether they have any suggestions that might help.

However, twins who are happy and are able to allow each other separate friends and separate outings, can have a great deal to gain from being at school together, giving each other support when needed.

10
Parenting

When to become involved

Twins in this age group generally play well together, but most twins have disagreements, at least occasionally. Those who have learned that parents will willingly involve themselves in their battles and that complaints against their twin will be instantly investigated are less likely to sort out their problems for themselves. Like all brothers and sisters, they need to find their own pecking order. In any case it can be difficult to tell who struck the first blow, either physically or verbally.

When parents have to step in because of something that the twins have done, such as throwing a ball through a window, both twins may deny responsibility. It's possible that one twin may have encouraged the other, rather like hiring a hit man. He may prefer to play safe himself, but is delighted to live through the more adventurous twin. Sometimes the incident may be typical of one of the twins so that an inspired guess can be made as to who was responsible. If this is not possible and the twins were clearly together at the time, then they have joint responsibility and both should be dealt with in the same way. Owning up should always be praised. However, just as the culprit may deny the offence, so may an innocent twin claim responsibility in order to lessen the punishment for both.

Twins can provoke each other by playing on each other's weaknesses. In this way the co-twin is used as a means of attracting the parents' attention, whilst the one that set him up appears to be the 'good' twin. Twins whose parents have learned not to respond to similar bids for negative attention will be less likely to be provoked. Both twins may sometimes provoke another child in the family in the same way.

The more twins develop as individuals, the less likely they are to act in concert and push each other into set roles. The fairer the parents, the more likely the twins are to develop an honest response without fear of parents overreacting.

Time

Twins need time to talk to their parents, not only about their worries and fears, but also about practical day-to-day things.

If they each have a separate bedroom this can easily be arranged and ten minutes allowed for each child at bedtime. If they sleep in the same room, then each child can spend ten minutes talking with the parent in another room. Children will often try to overrun their time, but it is up to the parent to be firm. Children can accept a time limit more easily if they know there will be other opportunities to have the parent to themselves. For example, each can take it in turns to go out shopping with one parent whilst the co-twin stays at home with the other.

If it is clear that something is worrying one of the children, then space should be made to allow him to talk about it. Twins can often find it difficult to give each other time on their own with parents, but if they find that they are also given time when they need it they will be more tolerant. Care has to be taken that the privilege is not abused, so that one twin begins to feel shut out.

As twins get older, finding time for each of them becomes easier because they begin to develop their own individual interests and friends and are not always together.

Favourites

In Part Two we talked about early bonding and the development of a twin preference. This preference may fade as children grow older, though it can persist. Sometimes the original preference is forgotten and a new one develops because of a similarity in character or interests. Whatever the reasons, it can make mothers, and sometimes fathers, feel guilty and they may try to make it up to the less-preferred twin. It is far better to accept the preference as a fact of life and then just get on with parenting them, and loving them, than to try and compensate, which can then lead to the unequal parenting we have been trying to avoid. Guilt can sometimes make loving difficult.

Equality

Not only can we feel guilty if we don't love them equally, but also if they don't achieve equally.

When there is a difference in age, differences in ability or achievement can be accepted more easily. If it's the younger child who has a particular skill, the older one may still be ahead because of his years. On the other hand, the older child's interests and seniority may make comparisons less likely. In the last resort parents may say, 'Well, they're two individual children and they have to accept their differences.' This is not to say that it won't cause problems; it may still do so.

Where twins are concerned, of whatever type, we find it harder to take a long-term view. If we could find it easier to accept their differences ourselves, instead of trying to make things fair, the children might find it easier too. They would then perhaps allow each other their own individual achievements without hoping that we could wave a magic wand so that they, too, could swim a length, or play a tune, or do a sum like their twin.

Unfortunately even if parents have encouraged individual achievement, twins, particularly identical twins who often dislike competing with each other, may feel some guilt if one succeeds where the other fails. The twin who has failed may be happy for the co-twin's success, or, on the other hand, double the successful twin's guilt by coping badly with failure.

It is important that parents do not identify too strongly with the feelings of either twin. Twins should not be encouraged to feel that it is enough for one to succeed if both have the ability. Similarly, failure should be seen as success delayed, or as an opportunity to try an alternative route. The more twins seek to attain identical goals, in whatever sphere, the more they will be compared, or compare themselves. Diversity should be encouraged, but not insisted upon, within shared abilities and gifts.

We should encourage all children to achieve their potential, but it's their potential, and it does not have to be synchronized. It's quite likely that they did not take their first step at the same moment in time, so why should we expect them to be in step throughout their childhood with other achievements?

It's not fair

Twins often place great pressure on parents to make things fair. This can mean dividing the piece of cake exactly down the middle, saying whose turn it is to sit on the swing or behind the driver's seat, or making sure they each have the same number of sweets. New items of clothing may be demanded at the same time, although it may be only one twin who has a hole in his jeans.

This pressure can be very difficult to resist, partly because twins may make a fuss, a form of attention-seeking, and partly because it makes us, as parents, feel needed and important. But children's decisions are best left to children. Only if they directly affect the adults should parents step in. For example, if twins are squabbling in the back seat, driving may become dangerous and parents may have to sort out the argument. This may be by telling them both to be quiet! But if twins are arguing about the number of turns they've had on the swing, this should be worked out between themselves and parents should avoid becoming involved.

Tips for peaceful car journeys are: plenty of stops along the way, car games, small snacks and a reward for good behaviour at the end of the journey. Car seatbelts for children not only help to prevent accidents, but also help to keep them in their seats and out of each other's way!

Labelling

Twins, like other children, can very easily get stuck with a label. Sometimes together:

The clever twins
The musical twins
The silent twins
The difficult twins
The noisy twins
The terrible twins

or separately:

The tidy one
The stupid one
The thin one

The naughty one
The clumsy one
The talkative one

In Walt Disney's *Snow White* we can tell the seven dwarfs apart by their labels, 'Sleepy', 'Dopey', 'Sneezy' etc., and twins are often labelled for the same reason.

As we have seen from the Couple Effect, twins tend to allocate tasks within the twinship and may stress their differences. These differences can sometimes lead to labelling. Parents can make it easier, or more difficult, for twins to exchange tasks or borrow them from each other as they might a sweater.

How can parents prevent labelling?

We have seen how placing twins in different classes in school can help to prevent educational labelling. Both then have the freedom to develop all their interests and abilities and fewer comparisons are made between them.

Praise is the best way of encouraging good qualities in our children. Getting upset and angry is a negative way of rewarding behaviour which then makes it more likely to be repeated. Parents may also encourage certain behaviours by drawing attention to them because they see them as a way of individualizing twins. Small differences between twins can become big ones if they are exaggerated. For example, if one child has a tendency to fall over or drop things, parents can increase the likelihood of it happening again by making a fuss about it: 'There he goes again, coffee all over the carpet!' The child then sees 'being clumsy' as his task, as a way of expressing his own individuality and as a way of drawing attention to himself. Praise for successful attempts at control, rather than dwelling on difficulties, will build up a child's confidence, enable him to be more successful and prevent labelling.

Labelling one twin may push the other into an opposite way of behaving. Labelling one twin as 'good' can make it difficult for the other to get attention for good behaviour. He is forced to rely on other methods. On the other hand, labelling one child as 'naughty' can make it difficult for the other to let go and express feelings of anger or frustration. He may become over-controlled and tense. Pairs of brothers and sisters can sometimes be influenced in the same way.

Standing firm

Children of all ages need to know their own family rules and what to expect if they forget them.

Perhaps the most important rule for every child is that he must tell his parents where he is going, who he is going to play with and if there is any change of plan. Parents knowing where their children are means security for children and peace of mind for parents.

When parents are angry they can often threaten punishments that are difficult to carry out. For example, if a child has failed to tell his parents that he's going to a friend's house after school, he may be told that he will not be allowed out after school for a whole week. After two or three days the child may have become so bored and irritable, and is making life so impossible for his parents, that they give in and the child goes out to play. Once parents have given in, children become more powerful. They have found out that they can make their parents change their minds. When they are twins, the pressure is greater.

Moderate punishments, such as, in this case, keeping the child in the following day, usually work best. Children have a natural sense of fairness and really prefer to have limits set, however much they may complain!

A child who finds that his parents will give in if pushed can feel unprotected and insecure. Imagine a house with sliding walls that give way when you lean against them. That's how it can feel to a child who is out of control. He may test his parents, not only to find out where the limits are, but also as a cry for help to them to set limits.

It's confusing for twins if parents are not in agreement about how they should behave, and they may play one parent off against the other. It's worth setting aside a little time to decide on what is important and the best way of encouraging twins to respect their parents' decisions. Like other children, they can be very good at calling our bluff if we are not convinced that we are doing the right thing. It's better to have a few rules that both parents can agree on than a lot of rules on which they cannot agree.

Children will do anything to make parents change their minds, if they think that they will be successful. They will whine, argue and even be physically violent. If both twins are behaving in this way, it is a brave parent who can withstand the pressure. Anything for a quiet life. Unfortunately life becomes anything but quiet! If toddler habits of behaviour have not been outgrown, a child of eight may still be resorting to temper tantrums if he finds that they get results. At eight, they can be harder for both the child and the parents to control.

Even if parents only give in occasionally, this is enough to make it worthwhile putting on a performance. The child may think that it just requires a bit more over-acting to get the parents to give in. Even if parents don't change their minds, they may eventually become so upset and angry that they reward the behaviour with negative attention. Negative attention, as we saw in Part Two is a reward in itself, and children learn which behaviour produces the best results. It's a natural learning process and children learn fast!

On the other hand, although twins sometimes encourage each other to take risks and break rules, they often need less reminding than other children because they act as each other's conscience. Also, because twins are sometimes slower in learning social skills and may lack confidence, they often rely more heavily on their parents than other children. This can make them more willing to accept parental authority and avoid confrontation.

Explanations

Some parents feel that if children understand why they may not do something, then they will naturally make the right choice. Though simple explanations are useful and helpful to children, particularly twins who need to be encouraged to ask questions, lengthy explanations can become rewarding in themselves and encourage, rather than discourage, the behaviour. One twin may use this as a method of monopolizing the parent's attention. It would be a perfect world if we all behaved as we should because we knew that it was sensible!

Sometimes one twin may be a child who lacks confidence. Mole-hills can become mountains and parents may find themselves continually soothing an over-sensitive or over-anxious child. Too much attention on these occasions can increase the symptoms of anxiety because the child learns that it gets a rewarding emotional response. Sympathy, without fuss, and gentle encouragement are best. This ensures that one twin is not pushing the other off stage.

One warning and time out

If one or both twins misbehave, they should be given one warning in much the same way as for the under-fives, but the response need not be immediate. For example: 'If you don't go up and get washed and undressed straight away, you'll have to go to bed fifteen minutes earlier tomorrow.'

Time out in the bedroom can give space for frayed tempers to be restored. Not more than ten minutes at any one time. If, when allowed out, the behaviour is repeated, then they are returned to their room. Like the under-fives, older twins may decide to occupy themselves in their bedroom, but, so long as they have permission to come down when they are ready, there is no reason why they should have to stop. The aim of the exercise is to show the child that the behaviour will not get him any attention and to help him to regain control by himself. Time out, not punishment. It also helps the parent to avoid confrontation and possible loss of control.

Praise for twins when they are successful is essential if they are to learn to control their own behaviour and work towards getting positive attention. We all love to be praised, and the more we are praised, the more we want to please.

Rewards are more enjoyable for everyone and children may respond well to being allowed to stay up later at the weekend if they have gone to bed without a fuss, or with only one warning, all week. Another example might be to tell the twins that if they settle down to their homework without a fuss, they will be able to watch their favourite TV programme or go out for a game of football with their friends. Much more positive than, 'If you don't settle down to do your homework you will not be allowed to watch the TV programme.'

Helping

Twins, like other children, need to be encouraged to help with household tasks. They may make double the work, but they can also be double the help. It may often seem quicker to do it yourself when twins of any age are learning a new task, but this is a short-sighted policy and can lead to the labelling of twins as unhelpful.

If a child is encouraged to help he may well put more effort into the task than the parent: shining taps, for example. The six-year-old making jam tarts may turn into the teenager who gives the parent a rest from making dinner.

If twins learn that parents will always do things for them, they may not learn to do things for themselves, or for parents, and they will find it difficult to take responsibility and grow up.

Sometimes one twin may do a task better and quicker than the other. This can result in specialization. If one twin gives up and allows the other to get all the praise, he will be labelled 'the unhelpful twin'. When this happens it can be useful to give each child his own tasks, praise effort and avoid comparisons.

Parents often complain that their children are untidy and parents of twins are no exception. If twins share a room and one is tidier than the other, this can create problems. They will usually draw an imaginary line down the middle of the room, each keeping to his own territory. However, it is usually the parents who become most annoyed and the more they nag, the worse it seems to get. Negative attention again!

If the twins' room needs cleaning, then an easy way out can be to put everything on their beds and let them put their own things back as they would like. Another tip is to have a rule that the room has to be tidied before friends are invited in.

When twins are young, they can often be overloaded with toys and this can be one of the reasons why their bedroom may become difficult to tidy. If toys are rationed, children enjoy them more and the problem is reduced. A star system can be particularly useful in helping twins to put away their clothes and belongings.

Many parents find that as their twins grow up they become an invaluable pair of helpers.

The older child

As we have seen from the section on 'Family Relationships', older children can sometimes feel isolated and unloved. This can result in attention-seeking behaviour both at home and at school. Usually it is within acceptable limits, but it can occasionally disrupt the

family. On the other hand, older children can often be a great support to parents and twins alike and develop very special qualities.

Time with parents is important for the older child who may have lost so much of theirs to the twins. Time in the evening, after the twins have gone to bed; time to talk about what he has done at school before the twins tell their news; time with each parent on their own for a little while at weekends, and occasionally time with both parents without the twins, to do something special and grown up. Grandparents, too, can be very important to the older child, and there is often a close relationship, particularly if he was the first grandchild.

Most parents are well aware of possible trouble spots and make a special effort to help the older child. However, they can sometimes feel helpless if the child sends out his signals for help by continuously misbehaving.

Apologizing

Getting children to apologize can result in a fight to the death, both parties being determined not to lose. It can be used by children as a marvellous piece of negative attention-seeking, though there are some children who will apologize quite easily. If the parent can honestly say that if they were in the same situation they would offer an apology, then this is probably the occasion when the child should apologize.

The star system

When a child has got locked into negative attention-seeking, he may find it difficult to produce good behaviour. Only when alone with the parent, or parents, does the child find it unnecessary to produce bad behaviour because he has the parents' undivided attention. This can give parents a glimpse of what the child could be like and encourage them to help the child to become his best self.

One of the keys to unlocking good behaviour is the Star System.

The emphasis is on reward for good behaviour rather than penalties for bad behaviour. If parents have reached the end of the road, they have usually run out of penalties anyway: all pocket money has been stopped, the child thrives on negative attention such as smacking and shouting, and may seem uncontrollable. The child has given up working for positive attention. The parents, and the child himself, may find it difficult to see him in a good light.

First, all bids for negative attention, such as attempts at confrontation, arguments and bouts of temper, should be ignored as much as possible. No self-respecting actor would go on stage if there were no one in the audience and he never received any applause. All good behaviour should be praised. Quick hugs help to reduce the distance between parent and child if he finds it difficult to accept a cuddle.

Parents then decide together which two pieces of behaviour they would like to change. If both parents are available, this could be done after the children have all gone to bed in the evening. There may be a great many pieces of behaviour that they would like to change, but they should start with the two that they find most difficult to tolerate. Let's suppose they choose:

1 Not making a fuss about going to bed
2 Not hitting the twins

In order not to have the spotlight on one child in the family, two different pieces of behaviour are chosen for each of the twins and any other children who are neither too young nor too old to take part. Bedtimes might be chosen for them as well. Other possibles might be:

Getting up quickly in the morning
Making their beds
Tidying toys
Tidying their bedrooms
Feeding the cat
Clearing away the dishes
Laying the table

Charts are drawn up for each child with his name on the top. Three weeks will fit quite nicely on to one large page (see page 169). If parents feel that earning the stars is going to be quite difficult at first, days can be divided into mornings and afternoons and stars can be earned for each half of the day. Sticky stars can be bought at most stationers, or stars can be drawn in with a coloured pencil, a different colour for each of the two pieces of behaviour.

The chart should be pinned up on the kitchen door, or a similarly important place, and stars awarded by parents at the end of each day with plenty of praise. If both parents are not available, the other parent is told as soon as possible of the children's success when the children are there to enjoy seeing his, or her, pleasure. Failure is not mentioned.

Once a star is given it cannot be taken away for any other piece of bad behaviour, and when there is no star, the space should just be left blank. Parents may still decide that if there is too much fuss about going to bed, the child goes to bed earlier the next night or, if he starts hitting the twins, he has time out in his room. Children are always given one warning that if the unwanted behaviour continues they will not get their star. It is important that parents remain calm and do not become involved in giving the child negative attention such as shouting, smacking, arguing or getting upset. All attention should be gained by winning stars.

When the child has got five stars he earns a prize. Earning the stars may be difficult at first. He may earn one on Monday and then no more until Thursday, and he may not have earned all five until the end of a fortnight. It's not like Bingo: he doesn't have to have a complete line to earn his prize, he just has to have five stars somewhere on the page. Some parents give a gold or silver star for each fifth star that is won.

Prizes may be different for each child, or the same for all the children. They can be sweets, comics, inexpensive gifts such as cheap plastic toys, anything that the child would like and the parents can afford to give frequently. Prizes should always be small tokens, never expensive toys. It could be a way of the children earning pocket money.

Prizes should be awarded as quickly as possible after the five stars have been won. Parents who forget the prize can forget the star chart – it is unlikely to work! Prizes which are something that the child would get whether he earned his stars or not, will also not work. Only if sweets are a treat will sweets be valued as a prize.

After about three weeks, the child is usually having little difficulty in earning the stars. Two new pieces of behaviour can then replace the old ones which have become a habit. Gradually the stars can fade out as the child discovers that being good is more rewarding than being naughty, and he continues to get plenty of praise.

Parents are the best judges of how easily their children can earn their stars. For some children the target might be ten stars rather than five. If it's too difficult the child will give up, if it's too easy the child will not have a sense of achievement.

If parents are at all worried, it is often helpful to discuss their anxieties with a professional.

One of my twin boys is always arguing with me. Whatever I say, he always has an answer.

He may have found a way of getting your attention. Refuse to be drawn into arguments. If he disagrees with you, say that you're sorry but you don't intend to have a discussion, and remain firm. Bids for individual attention are quite usual, but try to make sure that they each have some time when they can talk to you on your own. Have some separate outings, even if it's only to the local shops.

One of our twins is much more sensitive than his brother and is easily upset. We find that we are letting him get away with a lot more because if we tell him off he reacts badly.

Sometimes the more sensitive twin was originally the less-preferred baby. If this is so you may have been trying to give in to him in order to redress the balance. Over-protecting him now will mean he is less able to deal with life's knocks as he grows older, so try to be a little firmer. He may have found a way of getting you to bend the rules for him. This can make things difficult for everyone in the family, including his twin. The other twin may feel that he's got to make up for his brother's sensitivity by being sensible and grown up when he might like to be more childish himself sometimes.

The sensitive twin may have a natural dislike of anger and shouting. There is no reason why he can't be dealt with quietly and calmly, but without being given more than one chance to do as you ask.

I find it very difficult to say this, but one of my twin daughters is very pretty with an attractive personality to match. The other is rather plain and has a chip on her shoulder. I am always telling her how pretty she is when she's dressed to suit her looks, but she prefers the same clothes as her sister which don't suit her at all. She adores her twin, but feels that she just can't compete.

This is a problem that is not just confined to twin sisters, but it does make the problem more difficult to deal with.

If it is at all possible in your area I would consider different schools, so that your daughter does not feel she is being compared with her sister. It's personality which counts, and you can help her to have a more beautiful personality by refusing bids for negative attention which her complaints about her looks may have become. Don't be drawn into long discussions about it, but ask her if she chooses her own friends because of their looks or simply because she likes them.

Give them both plenty of love and forget about their looks. The less you worry about it the less it will be of a concern to the twins. Treat them both alike and expect the same behaviour from both. Let her wear what she likes: choosing the wrong clothes may be another bid for negative attention. If you become less sensitive to it she may start to choose the clothes that suit her.

One of my twin girls always rubs me up the wrong way and we finish up having a fight. She gets on very well with my husband; it just seems to be me.

Once a child has found a way of getting attention, even if it's for the wrong reason, she will keep on using the same method. She probably spends more time with you than with your husband and is trying to find a method of getting even more of your time. The only way to stop it is to convince her that it will not get her the attention she is seeking. Walk out of the room if you find it difficult to keep your temper, but don't be a puppet with your daughter pulling the strings. Give her plenty of attention when she's being helpful and pleasant and find time to be on your own with each of the twins for a short while each day. Look for opportunities to give praise. If you can stick to this, you will be surprised to find how much nicer she becomes.

You don't say how old she is, but this type of attention-seeking often occurs in adolescence. You may find Part Four helpful.

My twin boys refuse to have time out in their bedroom and they are too big for me to make them go to their room. I don't know how to handle them.

I should tackle this in two ways. A star system, see page 113, to improve their behaviour, and the withdrawal of a privilege if they do not go to their room when told – missing a favourite TV programme, for example, or going to bed fifteen minutes earlier. If both parents are available when the privilege is withdrawn, it will be easier to see it through. Make it clear to them that time out is only for ten minutes and give them one warning that the privilege will be withdrawn.

My son is always using bad language. I don't know where he's got it from, certainly not from me. The twins are beginning to copy him, what should I do?

Ignore this bid for negative attention and award stars when he has not used bad language for a whole morning or afternoon. Perhaps he could earn his second star for helping in the house, clearing away the dishes, for example. Is he having some special times when he doesn't have to share you or your husband with the twins?

My daughter seems to think that money grows on trees and is always wanting us to buy her new things. She and the twins get their fair share, but she always wants more.

Your daughter probably feels that the twins are getting a lot of your time and attention and this is a way of getting more for herself. It also seems to have become a way of getting negative attention because she makes you feel guilty that you have not more to give and it's upsetting you. In fact, it wouldn't make any difference if you were a millionaire, she'd still be doing the same thing.

Try to leave the twins with someone else occasionally and take her out on her own. This is not in order to buy her something, except perhaps a Coke or an ice cream, but just to give her some time for herself. Be very firm when she asks for something and don't be drawn into a discussion about why she can't have it – she knows already! Find opportunities to praise her.

My twin boys are still wetting the bed. We've tried everything, but nothing seems to work.

There could be several reasons for this. A visit to the doctor will put your minds at rest that there is no medical reason.

Sometimes twins (or a single child) can feel that their parents are not in control, particularly if the children have to make all the decisions for them. They then believe that they are uncontrollable and that life is very unpredictable and that they are therefore unable to control themselves, which includes their bladders. Parents taking back the control and giving the children only the choices and decisions that are appropriate to their age can often prove successful.

Children who are under stress, either personally or because of difficulties that the family may be experiencing, can also wet their beds. The children may not improve until they are feeling more secure.

Children can become 'stuck' with bedwetting as a means of gaining negative attention. A star or reward system can be helpful, combined with the minimum of negative attention. But it will take time and it is very important to persevere even if it does not appear to be working within the first few weeks. Combine it with a star for something that they can attain easily, e.g. helping lay the table.

Some children seem to be immune to the call of nature and may need an alarm system to help them wake up. Talk to your doctor.

4

Adolescence and After

11
Identity

Identical twins

As we saw in Part Two, the identical twin is three months behind the non-identical twin in learning to recognize his own mirror image. This does not mean that having learned to recognize himself, he no longer makes mistakes. Many identical twins have told of their sense of confusion when they have looked in the mirror and for a moment believed that it was their twin who was staring back at them. Sometimes a mirror may be placed in such a way that one twin is reflected in it and the other cannot be seen. It may not be until the mirror refuses to reflect back the gestures of the unseen twin that he realizes that he is looking, not at his own reflection, but that of his twin. A variation on this theme is the story of Alice, aged nine, who was looking through the window of a parked caravan at what she thought was her reflection in a mirror, only to discover that it was her twin sister staring through the window on the other side!

Infant twins often respond to each other's names and for identical twins, who are so frequently mixed up, they may genuinely have some doubts as to who they are, for the boundaries between 'me' and 'him' are unclear. As they go through childhood, adults and other children will continue to be uncertain as to which one they are, often only being able to tell them apart by small physical differences, or differences in hairstyles and dress. However, family and childhood friends who are frequently in their company usually learn to respond to personality differences and do see them as individuals in their own right, although they may not always treat them as though they were.

If twins go to different schools, or follow separate interests, they may not admit to being one of twins. If friends meet the co-twin there will often be a case of mistaken identity. Twins may accept the false identity rather than bother with explanations or they may make a joke of it. The mistake suggests that they are interchangeable, that they have made no permanent mark of their own, that they have not got an individual identity.

It is through relationships that adolescents build up their sense of identity, particularly those with the opposite sex. Though twins may play tricks on girlfriends or boyfriends and there are often unintentional mix-ups, these friends usually respond more strongly to differences in character between twins and are quite definite about which twin they are attracted to. The twins themselves, fortunately, tend to be attracted to different types. Maybe they are looking for the missing piece of the 'jigsaw' which will be different for each twin. Even if two pairs of twins date each other, there will be differences in character that will decide who takes which partner. Sometimes both twins become attracted to the same person, but we will look at the reasons for this later.

All teenagers become self-conscious about their physical appearance, but when any supposed faults are constantly paraded in front of them by their identical twin, they may be more difficult to cope with. Many twins will adjust their hair or dress if they notice that the other's is out of place, but they can't adjust a nose or skin-type!

All through their childhood, twins are compared with each other and small differences are used to tell the difference between identical twins. The twins themselves may cling to these differences in order to assert their own identity: 'He's the musical one, I'm the one that likes painting.' But using physical cues such as 'the fatter twin' or 'the taller twin' may make the youngster see himself as too fat, too thin, too small or too tall, whatever is picked out as a marker. By using other signals such as colours, brooches, badges or hairstyles, parents can prevent an inaccurate body image in adolescence which may lead to inappropriate dieting, weightlifting, and feelings of inadequacy.

Twins may experiment with dress and make-up to achieve individuality and a separate identity from their parents, in the same way as other teenagers. It is particularly important that this is tolerated, within reason, because it's a harder struggle for twins. There may be certain rules about what is acceptable at school, and each family will have its own set of boundaries.

Adolescent identical twins may try to dress as differently from

each other as possible, and one may be much more acceptable than the other. However, it really is a joint decision as to which twin takes which role, and one can only be tidy and acceptable because the other is not. This is part of the Couple Effect.

Twins who lack confidence may cling to their joint identity and dress alike. They are then assured of a place within their group as twins, but perhaps would be unacceptable or unable to cope as singles. They may rebel against their parents in the way that they dress, but not against each other. On the other hand, identical twins may simply be so in tune that they choose the same clothes and hairstyles even when they are not together and have individual friends and interests. Research into separated twins has shown that twins who have spent years apart can arrive at their reunion in almost identical outfits.

Identical twins have a need to know who they are and that they are not just a carbon copy of someone else. Twins who have been helped to find an individual identity during childhood are in a stronger position when they reach adolescence to cope with the self-doubts and the struggle to find a positive self-image that beset all teenagers.

Non-identical twins

Similar looking non-identical twins may have some of the same problems that are experienced by identical twins. Others mix them up, and they may have difficulty in being seen or seeing themselves as separate individuals. They can sometimes get their own body image mixed up with that of their twin and have beliefs about themselves that are not borne out by reality. Even dissimilar twins may fall into this trap. They are perpetually comparing themselves, or being compared, with their twin, and differences may become exaggerated. One twin may feel that he can never be 'good enough' if his twin seems more handsome, more clever or more popular. He may either become depressed or only feel that he has a role when he's in the company of his twin and can bask in his reflected glory. The co-twin, who appears so confident, may also need to be with his twin to convince himself of his superior identity that might lack reality if he compared himself only with the larger group.

If one twin is at a disadvantage, or feels he is at a disadvantage, because of differences in appearance, character or skills, separate schooling can enable him to find himself in his own group of friends without measuring himself, perhaps literally, against his twin.

This brings us to the problem of differences in growth rates. Growth and puberty are genetically linked and brothers and sisters in the same family may not all be alike. This does not usually cause problems unless a younger child outstrips an older one. When there are two children of the same age, however, one may leave the other behind. The taller or more mature twin may have problems because others have higher expectations of him which he tries to fulfil, and his expectations of himself may be greater.

The later developer, who may look like a younger brother or sister and is often treated as one by his twin and others, may feel some resentment and try to attract attention to himself in other ways. However youngsters are often aware of the complications that puberty brings, mood swings and clashes with parents, and may be happy to prolong their childhood and bask in being 'the little one'.

(Although most smaller identical twins catch up with their co-twin as their genetic clock makes up time after being slowed up when they were still in the womb, a few may not. This can affect the division of tasks within the twinship.)

In the case of boys, height is usually seen as a measure of masculinity and a shorter twin may feel at a disadvantage. On the other hand, a bigger twin brother can sometimes prevent the bullying which is sometimes the lot of a smaller boy. Having a twin at the same school has its advantages!

If twins share the same bedroom and there is a time lag in the onset of puberty, this can be embarrassing to both twins. One has to come to terms with the changes that are taking place, the other may be self-conscious because of the absence of these changes. The youngsters will probably find ways of achieving privacy and these should be accepted without comment. If separate bedrooms are not possible, requests for a screen or curtain should be taken seriously.

For mixed-sex twins, adolescence can be a testing time as girls tend to mature at a faster rate than boys. A brother who has enjoyed a close relationship with his sister may have his self-image badly shaken if she starts dating older boys and doesn't want him around. His sister's bedroom becomes strictly private and confidences are shared with girlfriends. The twins' Secret Garden has a 'Keep Out' sign on the gate.

The boy from a mixed-sex pair may have doubts about his own masculinity and feel rejected and confused by his sister's mood swings. Fathers have an important role here in building up the boy's confidence by giving him the friendship and approval that will help him feel grown up and secure in his masculinity. Parents should also encourage the boy to pursue his own hobbies and interests. A part-time Saturday or evening job can be a great ego booster – a bit of cash in the pocket and a feeling of being part of the adult world. If there's no regular job available perhaps there are neighbours who would like their cars cleaned, some gardening done or who need a reliable baby-sitter.

The girl also needs to feel that her parents approve of her and accept that she is growing up. If mother and daughter can sometimes have outings together they will have opportunities to talk in a relaxed situation, and advice can be given when asked for. This will help to lay the foundations of an adult friendship.

Separate secondary schools can help to avoid some of the problems. The twins will feel freer to mature at their own rate, develop their own interests and make their own friends independently of their co-twin. They will then have less need to fight for that independence at home. However, many boys from mixed-sex pairs lead very independent lives, so that the changes which take place in their sisters' lives may be less important and separate secondary schools unnecessary. The girl might be a late developer, in which case the twins may keep in step with one another.

Nevertheless it can be useful for parents to be aware that when their daughter becomes a young lady, their son could have a problem coping with being a 'younger' brother and find his sister's older boyfriends difficult to accept.

Twins of all types may repeat the pattern of the parent couple within their own partnership.

One of my twins eats well but the other one looks like his shadow. He says he doesn't want to get fat like his twin brother, but I'm worried that he isn't eating enough.

It sounds as though eating well may be important in your family and most of us expect our sons to have healthy appetites.

If they are non-identical twins and only one is going through a rapid growth stage, one may grow taller and thinner than the other if they both eat the same. However, if they are both at the same stage of development they may be using their weight as a way of establishing their individual identities, particularly if they are identical twins.

First refuse to be drawn into any discussion about food and take no notice of how either twin is eating. It may have become a way of attracting negative attention. Then encourage other differences between the twins by suggesting that they have different haircuts and choose different clothes. Encourage as much separation as possible, both educationally and in their leisure time, so that differences in appearance become less important.

Try and get all the family to eat together. If necessary alter the times of the meals to fit in with the boys' activities and your husband's working day. Youngsters often eat better when they sit down and relax with the rest of the family and your husband can support you in not giving negative attention.

Sarah, one of my twin girls, always looks such a mess that I'm ashamed to take her out. Her room is always in a mess too. Her twin sister Jane is just the opposite. Sarah is hopeless about money, too. We give them both the same pocket money, yet she's never got enough and is always borrowing from Jane who is much more careful. I don't know how to get her to take more care.

This is a very good example of the Couple Effect. Jane is specializing in being tidy and careful, and Sarah in being untidy and careless.

Give Sarah no negative attention by nagging. Praise her whenever she is looking tidier or her room is in not so much of a mess. Make her feel good in other ways by encouraging her to help you with some of the household tasks and showing her that you're pleased with her efforts. Both girls could have their own special tasks. Try and spend some time with Sarah and Jane individually each day if possible.

One of my twins has plenty of boyfriends, but the other one, Susan, is always on her own. The girls used to do everything together. Susan is getting so unhappy and I don't know how to make things better for her.

Everyone is different. Let Susan mature at her own rate and don't be too worried about her. If she thinks that you are worried it will make her feel that she should be too.

Encourage her to join clubs and activities where she mixes naturally with boys. She probably has other friends at school who are not dating yet who she could invite home or go out with in a group. It's possible that she would be happier at a different school where she would not always be watching what her twin sister was doing.

Use this as an opportunity for your husband and yourself to get to know her on her own. Make the most of it, they grow up all too soon!

I have mixed-sex twins but my husband and I are divorced and are no longer in touch. My son is going through a difficult time because his sister doesn't want to be seen with him. They used to do everything together and always came home from school hand in hand.

Your son might be happier at a single-sex school, if that is available. He would be able to become more independent and not feel so rejected by his sister.

I understand that you are not in touch with your husband, but is it possible for your son to spend more time with a grandfather, uncle, or someone that he looks upon as a father figure, who can help to increase his self-confidence and make him feel grown up? You could help him by encouraging him to get a Saturday job and join a local club or activity group.

Have one afternoon each weekend, or perhaps one evening during the week, which is 'family time' when everyone makes himself free to spend some time together. Be quite firm about this and make it a bit of an occasion by making the meal a little more special on that day. The three of you could play a game or watch a video together, whatever the family likes doing. Friends could be invited home as well, as long as they are happy to be part of the family group on that day. This will help to prevent your son from feeling that he may lose his sister as he lost his father, and also help to give your daughter the family support that she needs.

12
Separation

Adolescence is a time when we rework the experiences of infancy, particularly those of separation. For many twins this is unfinished business. They may have learned to take their first steps away from mother, but hand in hand, so to speak, with their twin. Instead of the loved blanket or teddy bear, toddler twins have each other. But whereas the blanket or teddy are only objects, the co-twin can temporarily take the mother's place, giving instructions, being cross, or giving love. In this way those first steps towards independence can be undermined and separation is incomplete. Going to school may continue this experience: separation from mother, but still with the twin.

Twins may not be ready for the thrust towards separation until much later than their physical maturity would suggest, and parents who have quite decided that their adolescents have missed the 'difficult' stage altogether may find that it has only been postponed. So the adolescent twin, like a caged bird with the door open, may sense his need for freedom but lack the will to fly out, afraid of facing the world alone. Every encouragement is needed to help the bird flutter free with the door left open so that the return is not barred.

Twins are not the only children who may feel anxious about separating. Singles can also have difficulties for a number of reasons: early ill health, loss of a loved relative or long periods of separation from the mother figure. These may require the separation to be reworked in adolescence.

Separation from the twin

Those who have been helped throughout their childhood to develop as separate individuals may, by adolescence, have let go of each other's hands. It is often easier for non-identical twins who have acquired a greater sense of personal identity than for the identical twin who may have doubts as to whether he is complete in himself, or is one half of a whole. Similar looking non-identicals can have something of the same problem.

Those twins who have been together a great deal in childhood, particularly girls who are so often each other's best friend, may have difficulty in letting each other go. Just as in adolescence children go through a period of rejecting their parents in order to make the break, so can twins go through a period of rejecting each other and their twinness in order to separate. There are sometimes quarrels between the pair and complaints about being a twin, with the blame put on the parents. Accusations and emotional outbursts are often part of the adolescent scene and part of the reason for the anger may be fear of separating. The wise parent tries not to become involved in arguments or take accusations too seriously. Youngsters can be angry one minute and the best of friends the next.

Twins should be helped to find acceptable ways of separating by allowing each other to have friends of their own as well as those in common, and to have some separate leisure activities. Twins who are making each other, and everyone else, miserable may be happier in separate schools. It can be surprising to see the change when they come home from school actually pleased to see each other!

Some twins, particularly identical twins, may decide that they do not wish to separate and continue to do everything together. Others may separate a little within a close bond. Twins must do what is right for them. Possibly the happiest twins are those who are able to allow each other freedom to develop independently whilst continuing a lifelong friendship. There is no doubt that the relationship between identical twins can be a special one and a friend who instinctively knows how the other feels and thinks can be a marvellous companion. Some friendships between non-identical twins can also have this quality.

In the case of mixed-sex twins, as we have already seen, the girl may sometimes wish to separate when the boy may not. Both twins need sympathetic handling. The girl can have feelings of guilt about separating from her twin which can lead to an 'I don't care, I'll do what I like' attitude, and rejection of her twin. If parents can show that they understand her need for separation and give support to both twins, they will be helped to cope with their feelings. On the other hand, some girls may feel unable to separate from their twin brother because of feelings of responsibility for him. But it is not always the girl who wants to break away. It may be the boy who feels that he can only be himself if he is on his own with his own group of friends.

However it has been found that some mixed-sex twins are more similar to identical twins than to non-identical twins in their relationship and may have a natural sympathy and understanding that can survive separation.

Twins who have been very close, of any type, may have difficulty in accepting outside friendships in which they are not allowed to share. Many childhood friendships are ended because of the jealousy of the co-twin, or even because parents have been worried that one twin was being shut out.

In adolescence the search for a separate identity may lead to exclusive friendships with someone of the same or the opposite sex and, in the case of twins, the one who is excluded may feel unhappy and confused. He may do all he can to break it up, seeing the friend as a threat to the stability of the twin couple and perhaps to his own identity. Identical twins, and sometimes non-identical twins, may compromise by sharing the friend, or the date if it is someone of the opposite sex.

Twins generally start dating later than single children, though it will depend on how close the twin couple are. Twins are often shy, or may simply not be ready for dating. Other youngsters can feel uneasy about intruding on the twinship or uncertain about which one to choose. The sight of two identical-looking girls sitting side by side can be quite unnerving for some boys. Twins may feel more confident being together, but they are more likely to receive attention – as opposed to attract attention – if they separate. On the other hand twins can find it easier to make relationships with the opposite sex because they are used to sharing and being one of a pair.

Separating from parents

Twins tend to retain a childlike quality for rather longer than single youngsters. Perhaps this is because they have shared their

childhood with someone else and it is less easy to leave it behind, but it may also be due to the slight immaturity of language which can serve to retain the shared Secret Garden of infancy. Twins can often be refreshingly direct and have little use for humbug.

As we have seen, the twin's relationship with his mother is linked in babyhood to his co-twin. Separation from mother is never complete, his twin is his umbilical cord. There may also be feelings of jealousy which make him unable to leave her to his rival.

These feelings can still be around in adolescence.

Twins tend to make decisions by committee and if parents are often co-opted on to the committee, then separation may mean an inability to make decisions. Teenage twin girls, in particular, tend to think out loud, often using their parents to talk through feelings and ideas, competing with each other for talking time.

During adolescence the teenager usually goes through a period of rejecting his parents' values in order to declare his independence. The values he chooses are usually those of the teenage group to which he belongs. Twins, who often act as each others' conscience, may have difficulty in rejecting the values of their parents when they have been continually reinforced by their twin throughout childhood.

Twins are a group within a group and may not wish to exchange their values for those of others. They know they're right, their twin agrees! They have a tendency to be rather conservative, with a small 'c'. Husbands and wives often reinforce each other's viewpoints in a similar way. Twins are therefore less likely to challenge their parents' decisions which they feel are basically right.

Twins who have used their twin group constantly to undermine their parents' decisions will continue to reject their parents' authority in adolescence. However they only have the power if they stand together and this can make it more difficult for them to separate from each other. Apart, they are less powerful. It also makes it difficult for them to separate from their parents as they may be continually testing them out in an effort to find out where the boundaries of control lie. They become dependent on the negative emotional response of their parents.

If one of the twins has come to rely on negative attention, either because of bad behaviour or emotional problems, not only will he find it difficult to break out of the vicious circle, but his co-twin may as well. The co-twin's role is to be the 'good' twin, the one on whom the parents can depend. Rejection may be out of the question.

The often fragile identity of the twin can also make it difficult for him to risk rejecting a part of his own identity, the part which is supported by his relationship with his parents. Research has shown that the typical adolescent rejection of parents is often not found in twins: problems in adolescence are more likely to be those connected with identity than rejection of the parents' authority. Identical twins, who may be closer to each other than to their parents, may do their rejecting together. Certainly if twins wish to challenge their parents they usually find that they are more successful when they support each other.

Twins whose parents have joined the twin group may find themselves in an almost impossible situation; they can neither separate from their twin nor from the parent.

Even if parents have not joined the twin group they can find it very difficult to let go of their twins as they may have benefited in many ways from having twins in the family. There is a saying that 'if you want to make friends you should get a dog', but twins will act as an excellent substitute, though they can't be bought at the local pet shop! Parents who may never have seen themselves as in any way 'special' may change their view of themselves when they have twins. It can be difficult adjusting to children growing up and leaving home, but when those children are twins some of the glamour goes with them. Twins also demand extra skills and parents may feel at a loss when it seems these are no longer needed.

Parents who want to help their twins to let go are advised to prepare themselves well in advance, rather like preparing for retirement. The focus of attention can be shifted slowly from the twins to other interests and hobbies as the twins become more independent. If parents have allowed themselves their own space as the twins and other children have been growing up, it will be easier to find activities that they can share when the teenage children are busy with their own lives.

Twins who have been treated, and respected, as individuals and who have been encouraged to do things separately as well as together, will have the confidence to grow up and become people in their own right.

Many twins keep in close touch both with their twin and their parents, and sometimes with their twin through their parents.

Our twins are constantly quarrelling and fighting with each other. Life is impossible.

They are probably trying hard to separate and need all the help that they can get. Do they have separate rooms? This may be difficult, but it is often better for each to share with another child than to spend every hour of the day and night with each other. They need space to be on their own. Encourage them to join different clubs and have different interests. Take each twin out on his own on a regular basis. They would probably find it a lot easier if they were at different schools or colleges, though this may not be possible in your area.

One of my twins stays in her room all the time and is always crying. Now she doesn't want to go to school. I keep asking her what's the matter, but she says she doesn't know.

First of all take her to the doctor and have a thorough checkup. If there is nothing wrong, talk to her teacher and find out if there are any problems at school, either with work or friends.

This is a time when some girls can feel sad without any special reason, but it's important that she goes to school regularly or she will have a genuine reason for becoming worried or depressed.

Try not to get upset too, or get into long discussions, as this is a way of giving negative attention and can make it more difficult for her to be cheerful. She may be feeling very uncertain about herself. Ask for her help and advice and give her some special responsibilities. Show her that you appreciate what she has to offer. Encourage her to do more out-of-school activities.

My fifteen-year-old twins get annoyed so easily if their meal isn't ready on time or their clothes aren't ironed. There seems to be no pleasing them.

It sounds as if your twins are a very close pair and they've discovered that they are more powerful when they work together. Help them to separate by taking back some of the power. They are old enough to iron their own clothes, and this could be one of their tasks. And the meal should be on the table when it suits *you* not them. It can be very helpful if both parents work together as two parents can often support each other in being firm.

The twins are old enough to make a meal themselves sometimes and might enjoy it if they were given the opportunity. Perhaps they could take it in turns to prepare a meal at the weekend – one at a time, not both together. The rest of the family, including the co-twin, could go for a walk or amuse themselves in some other way for half an hour before the meal is served.

Twins, as with single children, can sometimes make us feel guilty that we're not doing enough for them, but it's important that they are given the chance to do things for themselves.

13
Parenting

All adolescents go through physical and emotional changes which affect relationships within the family. They can be up one day and down the next. They can be difficult, argumentative and moody, or delightful, helpful and friendly all in the space of the same week.

Adolescents tend to look at life through a magnifying glass. The singer is not just a singer, but a 'pop idol', clothing is often extreme, friendships are intense. Those whom they don't like may be seen as enemies. Feelings within the family are also magnified. Past jealousies and resentments may now be expressed 'times ten' and parents of twins can experience considerable guilt at what they appear to have done to their adolescent children. The more they try to placate them, the worse it seems to get. It's helpful to remember that even adolescents who are not twins or who have not got twins in the family, often accuse their parents of being uncaring or of not loving them enough. If parents do not allow themselves to become upset by these and other accusations, they will be ready for the same child when he comes back, sometimes minutes later, in a different mood having quite forgotten what was said.

When the adolescent refuses to allow an argument to end or continues to reproach the parent or fails to get the message that his behaviour is unacceptable, he should be asked to go to his room. Alternatively the parent himself can pull out of the situation by going into another room or, if that fails, taking a walk around the block or going for a five-minute drive in the car. This shows the youngster that the parent means business and prevents the build up of negative attention. It does not mean that the youngster has 'won'. He has only won if he has succeeded in making the parent give him negative attention by getting angry, getting upset, or being drawn into an argument.

The older child who has shared his early years with the twins, may, like them, need to rework his early experience of separation.

But in his case it could be because he had to separate too much too soon, and finds the idea of loss frightening. He may return to toddler habits, tantrums and demanding bahaviour, which can result in rejection by his parents. This tends to reinforce his early experience. By not responding to bids for negative attention and giving the maximum of positive attention, the adolescent will be helped to find more acceptable ways of behaving which will not bring him so continuously into conflict with his parents. Praising a youngster who seems bent on provoking the parent can often be the most difficult step, but the youngster is so often one who lacks confidence that this is an essential ingredient to improving his self-image. He can then separate without rejection, and have greater confidence in himself and his ability to cope with whatever life may bring.

Twins are sometimes late arrivals in a family where there are already older children who are approaching, or who have already reached, adolescence. The children may be delighted at the idea of having twins in the family, but twins involve a lot of time and attention and there are few parents who can honestly say that family life has remained unchanged. A single baby can sometimes fit in with the life style of older children, but with two it is usually the other way round. Some older children will respond well to the challenge, others may become more demanding of the parents' time, attention, and often money.

Adolescents tend to be self-conscious and lacking in confidence, although this is sometimes disguised by showing-off, aggressive behaviour, or by exploiting their attractiveness to the opposite sex. Those who have found an acceptable way of being successful in adult terms, by being good at schoolwork, artistically or in the use of a practical skill, will have less need to assert themselves in other ways. Adolescents need approval as plants need the sun, and there is no one without a skill of some sort, although it may not be the one that the parents might have hoped for or expected. If children have aptitudes, parents can reinforce them by praise and encouragement, but they cannot create those that do not exist. Constant criticism, far from improving performance, will persuade a youngster that he can never measure up to his parents' expectations and he might as well give up. Clearly a job badly done does not deserve praise, but a job willingly done does and so does a job that is performed better than the time before.

Adolescent twins are continually comparing themselves and being compared by others. They may deliberately choose to follow different interests, subjects and careers in order to assert their differences when their preferences may be very similar. The less that twins are subject to comparison within the home and outside it, the greater their freedom of choice. The quality of any given task should be judged against their own best, not that of their twin. The advice on giving praise included in Part Three applies equally to the adolescent group. They need to know when they have done well and feel that their parents are proud of them.

Being grown up is a two-way process. It means being given more independence and freedom on the one hand, and more responsibility on the other. Youngsters need to be given responsibility not only for doing some of their own tasks – making their own bed, tidying and cleaning their own room – but also others around the home. They can then feel that they are accepted as adults and are making their own contribution. This might be linked to extra pocket money, if they have not got a part-time job, or extra privileges. But just as parents like their contribution to be appreciated, so does the youngster. No one likes to be taken for granted!

Adolescents are usually very self-centred. Finding out who they are means finding out about *their* bodies, *their* feelings, *their* relationships and, of course, about *their* needs. These may not take into account those of the parents. Parents also have rights, and the adolescent has to learn to respect these if his own are to be respected.

Adolescents need time on their own with their parents, and the importance of separate bedtimes for twins and older child cannot be over-stressed. Twins may exert a great deal of pressure to be allowed to stay up as late as an older brother or sister, but if this can be resisted the time can be of great value both to the older child and to the parents. When the children are very close in age, their interests will usually ensure that there are some times when each child is on his or her own with the parents.

Some older children may join the twin group and have difficulty in separating because they feel that they cannot abandon the group or because the twin group contributes to their own sense of identity. These children are often very caring and may maintain a long and close relationship with the twins, even when they themselves marry and have a family of their own.

It is difficult to break away from parents to whom you are close and the adolescent often has feelings of guilt. For this reason the magnifying glass may be used to exaggerate parents' faults and attitudes in order to justify breaking away – parents who are too understanding can actually make the process more difficult. Parents who seem unlike the 'ideal' parents presented by the media or decided upon by the larger adolescent group to whom the child belongs may be criticized. Many adolescents become so self-conscious about themselves, that this self-consciousness is enlarged to include the parents, who become a constant source of embarrassment to the teenager. This can be a testing time for parents, particularly if they begin to look at themselves and each other through the adolescent's magnifying glass. Compromise and tolerance are as essential between parents as they are between parents and adolescent, and parents can set an example that is well worth passing on.

Privacy is an important part of separateness and this is often difficult to find in a family with twins. Children need to learn to respect each other's space, both physical and psychological. Twins often seem to respect physical space – this is your side of the room, this is mine – but may disregard the need for psychological privacy, not only of each other, but also of brothers and sisters. They will often tell the parents about how another child in the family is getting on, both inside and outside school. Though reassuring for the parent, it can be upsetting to the brother or sister. Parents, too, need their privacy if they are to develop their own relationship.

Parents and children are preparing for a new phase of life and may experience similar feelings of loss for what has gone before and anxiety about what lies ahead. They may even both be experiencing physical changes. This is a time when parents value the support of partners, family and friends, and may understand the adolescent's need for friendships, although they are not always the ones that the parents would have chosen for him.

The adolescent, uncertain of his identity, seeks special friendships as mirrors in which to find himself. Problems can arise when an exclusive friendship may seem to threaten the identity of the twin who is on the outside. Adolescents do not always take a long-term view, and it may seem to the twin who is left out that he is about to lose his twin for life. Parents can be swept along on the tide of his fear and insist that he is included in the friendship, which becomes a threesome.

Eventually one twin may wish to marry or form a permanent relationship. Most parents would like to see their twins form a new partnership, but if the first attempts at forming a special friendship fail then it becomes progressively more difficult and frightening. Parents should give their approval to new friendships, rather than add to the feelings of guilt that the youngster is probably experiencing, and encourage the other twin to find friends of his own.

Amongst same-sex twins, discarded friends may become the friend of the other twin or they may be deliberately poached causing bad feelings between the pair. There is little that parents can do. Identical twins often seem to have a need to share everything with their co-twin and may even deliberately have encouraged the transfer. Some identical boys share their girlfriends, the girl occasionally believing that she is only going out with one of them if the twins are used to playing tricks of identity. This happens less frequently in the case of identical girls, though they may go out in a threesome. However if twins of both sexes are helped to respect each other's property and privacy as they are growing up, hopefully they will also respect each other's friendships.

It is just as important that 'no' means 'no' for this age group. Adolescents will push parents to their limits and it is much easier if they know just where these limits are, though they may be negotiable. It can often be difficult for a youngster to say 'no' when he's out with his friends and it can help if he can blame his parents and not lose face. He also continues to need a framework in which he can exercise an increased amount of freedom. The adolescent needs to feel safe, and he won't feel safe if he's given too much freedom too soon.

The trouble with adolescents is that they are adolescents. In other words, they are children some of the time and young adults some of the time and nobody knows, least of all the youngster, which it's going to be at any given time. The youngster is often resentful at being treated like a child when he thinks he's being grown up, or vice versa, but it's impossible for parents always to get it right.

Parents need to be consistent in giving love, even if the adolescent sometimes rejects it, and consistent in setting limits, even if the youngster sometimes resents it. The wise parent knows that the happiest children are those who are neither rushed too quickly into adulthood, nor discouraged from taking on the responsibilities and decisions that are appropriate to their age and maturity.

Most parents have a good relationship with their adolescent twins. However, as we have seen, a less confident twin can resort to attention-seeking behaviour which can split the pair into the 'good' twin and the 'bad' twin. Both then get locked into the parents, the one by having to remain as a support and unable himself to indulge in rejecting behaviour, the other because he is caught in an immature emotional vicious circle that he cannot break. The deadlock can only be broken by using similar methods to those that have been suggested for the younger age groups. The minimum of fuss and withdrawal of attention for negative attention-seeking and the maximum of praise for acceptable behaviour. Individual time with both adolescents is essential so that fears and worries are not bottled up. Commonly twins take it in turns to be the 'good' twin, but they may sometimes get stuck.

Parents should avoid being drawn into discussions about physical appearance – none of us is perfect – but should tell their twins when they are looking smart or attractive. Crash dieting should be avoided: a sensible balanced diet is best, and regular family meals help to keep the lines of communication open. Mealtimes are often the only times when all the family meet together. Mealtimes should be as relaxed and enjoyable as possible. Table manners are best treated with the minimum of attention, but parents don't have to listen to a youngster with his mouth full; he can wait for a hearing until he's ready to talk, and not eat at the same time.

Teenage twins can be very persuasive if they have both decided that they want to go to a disco or a pop concert, or some other leisure activity, but parents often feel that there is safety in numbers and may allow them to stay out later or go to a party so long as they are together. They know that their twins are less likely to

misbehave when they have their 'minder' with them and are less vulnerable. However, this can also make it more difficult for twins to break away from each other and may reinforce their feeling that it is not safe to be alone.

Twins, like all adolescents, are often particularly good at making parents feel guilty or anxious in order to get what they want. (Parents are sometimes quite good at it too!) For example, mothers can often find it difficult to know whether their teenagers are really suffering from some vague illness and should not go to school (or college) or whether they are just trying to get some extra time at home. A good guide is whether they make a remarkable recovery every Friday evening, only to have a relapse on Sunday night or Monday morning. If they can go out with their friends on Saturday, then they are fit enough to go to school on Monday. Always check with the doctor, though.

There may be other reasons why they want to stay at home, such as separation for the first time from their twin or difficulty in coping with work, or both. College may be the first experience of separation for some twins and it may take them rather longer to settle. It sometimes helps if they can visit each other so that they can have a mental picture of where the other twin is and what he's doing so he doesn't feel so cut off. A great deal depends on the individual twin. Adolescents are also very sensitive to any difficulties that parents may be having and may respond to the parents' needs.

Some twins, particularly boys, may be less skilled in language and become self-conscious about saying what they think or feel, especially if the rest of the family finds it very easy. How can you explain to your parents why you should be allowed to do something if they are much better at telling you why you can't? In family discussions it may be easier to say nothing than look foolish in front of the others. Some boys may say, 'I don't know', or 'I can't remember', when they know the answer, but it's too much trouble to put it into words or risk being made fun of by a bright younger sister. Boys will usually say what they want to say, but when they are on their own and feel safe and have had time to think it over. A single child who feels less skilled in language than other members of his family may behave in a similar way.

Parents sometimes have unfinished business from their own adolescence. They may feel that they were never able to do many of the things that they would have liked to have done at the same age and may either try to push their children into fulfilling their own unfulfilled dreams and ambitions, or take a change of direction themselves. Sometimes there is a fear that children will repeat their parents' mistakes and they may try so hard to prevent them that they succeed in doing exactly the opposite.

Children have to be free to find their own path to adulthood: they are new people, not ourselves. When making rules for twins, parents should think of them as individuals and not treat them as any different from a single child. They need to know that we are there to turn to and to set guidelines. If parents become big brothers and sisters, accepting the adolescent's values, then the adolescent not only finds it difficult to reject his parents, but is also prevented from deciding for himself what he would like to keep of his parents' values and what he would like to reject.

Adolescent twins can be exhausting, worrying and demanding, but they can also be loving and rewarding.

I dread the phone ringing in case it's the school or a neighbour complaining about my twin boys. What can I do? They're too old for a hiding.

Get your partner to support you in setting limits. Have a family meeting and tell the boys exactly what will happen next time they misbehave and that they will only have one warning. Always carry out the threat, which could be not allowing them out for two evenings after school, missing a treat, stopping pocket money or a TV programme, whatever *you* decide. Have a few important rules that have to be kept and turn a blind eye to some of the smaller ones. Give praise when they do as you ask and when there have been no phone calls. You might consider separate schools as it may only be when they are together that they get into mischief. Are they in different classes?

I get on very well with one of my twins, but the other one deliberately does everything he can to make me angry. I've tried shouting at him and hitting him and stopping his pocket money, but it only seems to make him worse.

He seems to be getting a great deal of negative attention and may have got stuck in the 'bad' twin position. I would suggest the minimum of attention for bad behaviour. Refuse to become involved if he tries to make you angry. If necessary, walk out of the room. He may try even harder before he gets the message. Give him plenty of positive attention, praise him when he is helpful and pleasant. Individual time with each twin will help them both to develop as rounded individuals rather than being two halves of a whole with one having all the bad bits. Be consistent. Use the one-warning system.

Your son may be feeling overshadowed by his twin and is drawing attention to himself by his bad behaviour. Have you thought about separate schooling? I would certainly suggest separate classes if they are in the same class at school.

Our twin girls are as good as gold, but our older son is quite impossible. He is rude, aggressive and argumentative.

This problem is very similar to the last one and needs the same response. So long as you continue to give him negative attention he will keep trying to get it, particularly as he may feel that the twins are getting all the positive attention. He needs to feel that being the older child is special and important by having special privileges, for example staying up later, having more pocket money and having the occasional outing with both of you on his own. He should also have special responsibilities. Give him plenty of praise and positive attention and the minimum of negative attention. He may be going through a period when he finds it difficult to control his feelings and emotions and the twins may not yet have reached this stage. This can emphasize the difference between them and your son will need all the help he can get not to get things out of proportion.

One of our non-identical twin boys works really hard and is doing well, but the other one refuses to settle down to his homework and just sits glued to the television set. He's not stupid, he just won't try.

This may be the result of the Couple Effect; one's doing well so the other one feels that it's not his responsibility. On the other hand, he may not be quite as bright as his hard-working brother and may feel that second best isn't good enough either for himself, or for you.

Be firm about switching off the television for an hour or so each evening, whether he does his homework or not. Have a quiet talk with him about what he'd like to do when he leaves school and how he sees himself achieving it. If it's deep-sea fishing, fine, help him to find out all about deep-sea fishing. Make it clear that it's what *he* wants to do that matters, and that you will be quite happy with whatever he chooses. If you take the pressure off, he may decide to work at whatever he is interested in. Have a talk with his teachers at school and try to help them not to make comparisons, but concentrate on his good points.

Are they in separate classes? Have you thought about separate schooling?

My older daughter is always asking for new clothes and extra pocket money to go out with her friends. Money is tight now we have the twins, but if I refuse she says nobody cares about her and that we're always buying new clothes for them. I've tried explaining that they keep growing out of their old ones, but she doesn't want to listen.

She may be going through a time when she feels that everyone is against her and is particularly sensitive to the fact that the twins need so much of your time and attention. If she can't have your time then she'll have your money!

Don't allow her view of the world to colour yours. Concentrate on giving her special times after the twins have gone to bed and leave the twins with a friend or relation at least once a month and take her out by herself. You will then feel that you are giving her what she really needs, which is time, even if she still complains. Time is much more important than money or new clothes. Make her feel grown up by giving her extra responsibilities by which she earns her pocket money. If she does a particular task well, without making a fuss, perhaps this could earn her a little extra.

Every time my daughter gets a boyfriend, her twin sister Pauline takes him away from her.

If they are identical twins and have always been very close, Pauline may find it difficult to tolerate her sister having a friendship in which she does not share. If they are non-identical twins it's possible that there is some jealousy or competition involved.

Encourage as much separation as possible, educationally and socially, and spend time with each twin. Take them for outings on their own. Encourage your husband to spend time with each young lady as well; they may have got used to being in competition for his attention. Whether identical or non-identical, these two need to feel that they are important even when apart.

Our fourteen-year-old twins expect everything to be done for them and never lift a finger to help in the house. Shouldn't we expect them to do some jobs around the home?

It's what you would like them to do that matters. You may prefer to do things yourself, but on the other hand it can help children to grow up if they feel that they are contributing to the running of the home. Each child could have his own tasks for which he is responsible. If they are done reasonably promptly, without a fuss, they could earn extra pocket money. Write out exactly what is expected of them, so there can be no arguments and pin it up in the kitchen, but have a chat first so that each youngster has some say in the choice of tasks.

We've read through the book, but we've given up bothering about our thirteen-year-old twins. They do what they want to do, when they want to do it, and couldn't care less what we say. We've threatened all sorts of things but nothing works.

If you're happy with the way things are, fine. But it sounds as if they have managed to become very powerful and they are preventing you from doing some of the things that you would like to do.

Forget the threats and try the star system on page 113. They are not too old yet and it's surprising how collecting stars for a small prize can change the way that children behave. Once things have started to change, you may find it easier to be firm, using plenty of praise when they are successful.

14
Grown-up twins

Communication

We've talked about the way in which twins often make decisions by consulting their partners, much in the way that some married couples do, but in the case of twins it can be a lifelong habit born of their common culture. This can leave the grown-up twin a little at a loss when it comes to making decisions on his own. He may find it difficult to make up his mind and look for opportunities to discuss the pros and cons with someone else. The plus side of this is that twins can be very helpful when others have problems to talk over and make excellent counsellors and personal friends. However they do have to be on their guard against the feeling that others are slow in understanding the ideas that they are trying to convey. Singles do not necessarily have the sixth sense that twins tend to develop along with language, and so will need a little more time and patience.

Young men from same-sex boy pairs can find that they are uncomfortable in large groups and they tend to feel more at ease with just one or two friends. They may find it easier to do what they are best at, relating to people individually even within the larger group, than trying to compete with the crowd. However twins of all types may have experienced considerable popularity and special treatment as a result of being twins and see the world as a particularly welcoming and friendly place. This can give them a natural confidence, particularly when they are together.

Separation

Grown-up twins may continue to have difficulty in separating, not only from each other, but also from their families. We have seen how there can be a close tie between parents and twins partly based on the feeling that the twins can never get enough caring or loving.

This feeling can still be around in adulthood. Twins may not only wish to continue, and perhaps improve, their relationship with their parents, but may also wish to convince themselves of that personal approval which they might have felt was lacking as they grew up. Too great a separation could seem to leave the field clear for the co-twin, which may still be unacceptable. Lack of confidence in their own identity can also make it difficult for twins to operate singly and a parent may act as a substitute for the co-twin. Unfortunately relations and friends often continue to make comparisons between twins, so that whatever they do in life they are continually looking over their shoulder. They are constantly being asked about their co-twin as a parent might be asked about a child.

Unexpectedly the dependent twin may find it easier to strike out on his own than the dominant one, who can find it difficult to come to terms with the loss of his twin, rather as a mother often feels when her child starts school for the first time, or when the adult child leaves home. The dominant twin may put pressure on his co-twin to remain within the pair group or, if left on his own, could experience some depression. He may not be aware that he is going through a mourning period for the loss of his twin. He may also be unwilling to face the fact of the important role his twin held in his life – he is the strong one, he should be able to cope!

Marriage

Professor Zazzo has found that twins tend to marry rather later than singles, which he feels may be partly due to the special relationship that some twins have with each other. There is often a feeling of resentment against outsiders who threaten this intimacy and they may, in various ways, try to prevent it happening.

Identical twins who have been very close may find it difficult to walk out of the Secret Garden to find happiness with someone else. It may seem disloyal to abandon a childhood partner and they may identify with their twin's feelings of loneliness, of being left behind. Some may therefore make it a condition of the new partnership that the old one continues alongside, or may only be able to tolerate breaking away by putting considerable geographical distance between themselves and their twin. The feelings of the twin who is left can be a mixture of jealousy and loss, whilst the

twin that is forming the new partnership may experience a strong sense of guilt. After the first twin marries the second may marry quite quickly, but some may need time to work through their feelings and find a new identity.

A threatened twin from a close pair may deliberately sabotage the other's relationships, but sometimes adult friendships are shared, as childhood friendships have been, in order to maintain the balance of the twin couple. This is sometimes an acceptable solution, but it can lead to complications and upsets between the twins and may be confusing for the friends. A rare solution, but one that seems to work extremely well, is for twins to marry twins. An alternative is to marry a pair of brothers or sisters.

Twins who have tolerated each other's friendships in childhood, will find it easier to accept each other's boyfriends and girlfriends and will be happy, as well as sad, when their twin falls in love. Rather than attempt to destroy that relationship, they may try to find one of their own, or can feel free to pursue a career of their choice.

Twins tend to marry someone with a personality that is similar to their twin, although parents and brothers and sisters are sometimes used as models too.

Expectations that are brought to a marriage can be high. Most of us are hoping to find a soul mate, but may be prepared to accept something less. Twins, who for many years have lived with someone who understood their moods and feelings and who may have instinctively known what they were thinking or what they would like to do, may feel disappointed and cheated if their new partner fails to live up to their standards.

The fear of being alone can be greater for twins and help to prevent an early breakup of a marriage. This may give time for a greater understanding to develop. On the other hand, they may return, disillusioned, to the old partnership or continue looking for the ideal partner. If twins maintain the tie with their co-twin, where it is a strong one, alongside the marriage, there may be fewer emotional demands made on the marriage partner.

Twins who have been used to sharing each other's friends may find it difficult, sometimes, to tolerate a wife's girlfriends or a husband's pals. There may be attempts to undermine a friendship or else to share in it and turn it into a threesome.

Some husbands and wives can find it difficult to accept a close relationship between twins and try to separate them, or at least place limitations on the amount of contact between them. Twins need to be aware of their new partner's needs as well as that of their twin. Partners who feel confident that they come first will feel happier about the twin coming second.

The relationship between partners of a mixed-sex pair can differ a great deal. If the relationship has been a close one there may be difficulty in finding a marriage partner who can replace the twin. If the pair has been a rejecting one, this could make future relationships hard work. Although the girl of a pair may choose a partner similar to her twin, she should be on her guard against overprotecting him. He may not need it! However, if mixed-sex twins have been encouraged to have independent lives and interests, there is no reason why they should not have happy marriages, particularly as the nature of the opposite sex will be familiar to them and they may well bring a greater understanding to the marriage than many singles or same-sex twins. If twins of any type have been able to separate in adult life and make individual friends and relationships, then they will have acquired the experience and tolerance necessary to form a new partnership and perhaps have something to teach the rest of us!

Twins as parents

Twins who become parents have had little experience of a one-to-one parent/child relationship and may have a tendency to fall into a child/child relationship. Some twin parents find that they tend to group their children into pairs and feel that they do not need a great deal of personal time and attention. Many twin parents find that they have a special relationship with one of their children, either positive or negative, and relate to them as if they were their co-twin. Sometimes they may feel that another of their children seems similar to themselves, so that the two members of the twinship, with all that that entails, appears to be acted out in the next generation. Many parents find that their easiest children are the ones who are not the same sex as their twin. Mothers from mixed-sex pairs may be able to be consistent with their girls and encourage independence, but can sometimes over-protect their sons and find difficulty in being firm. Mothers from mixed-sex triplets can also have the same problem.

It's a tendency we all have to see our children as similar to other members of the family, our mother, brother and so on, and therefore to have preconceived ideas about their personalities which they often obligingly act out for us. However, it is important to realize that such similarities are superficial and that no child is a carbon copy of anyone else – twins, of all people, should appreciate this! Let children be free to be themselves and not grow up in the shadow of someone else's past, or have to work through other people's mistakes. Parents who are twins and have twins themselves need to be aware of this, particularly as many ideas about bringing up twins may have changed since they were children.

Friendship

One of the great pluses for twins, if they both get married or take up separate life styles, is the way in which they often grow closer.

They are less dependent on each other and the friction that sometimes appears in adolescence and young adulthood becomes less evident. Many brothers and sisters experience a similar improvement in their relationship, but with twins the lifting of the pressures of society and the support of others can enable them to reforge a very worthwhile and lasting friendship with their twin. Non-identical twins may be finally free of the 'twin' label. There will be a closer relationship between the children of a pair of identical twins because they will have more genes in common, so that friendships are often closer in the next generation. Curiously cousins are sometimes of similar ages, even to the month.

If twins of a pair who have stayed together are outward-looking they can become a very successful partnership, and if they enter into joint business or other ventures can prove that the pair is greater than the sum of its parts. Even twins who may be independent in every other way sometimes choose to work together because they complement each other so well. They may also use their joint resources in other ways, in sport for example, or to be of service to others. The special relationship that is so often a part of being an identical twin is perhaps best expressed by the elderly gentleman who had survived his first wife and married again and who had had a successful career: 'My greatest wish is to die on the same day as my twin brother.'

15
. . . And then there was one

The bereaved parents

The loss of a child at any stage brings heartbreak as there are so many might-have-beens, but the loss of a twin is somehow perpetuated in the survivor. There is also the loss of something that is not given to everyone: the privilege of having two babies, an achievement that is out of the ordinary.

The way that hospital staff react to the death of a stillborn or newborn twin is of great importance. The birth of twins in the maternity ward is always exciting and staff may deal with their own feelings of loss by denying those of the parents. They may also feel that parents should be grateful that they have one healthy baby when others, less fortunate, have none. The mother and father may be given the message that it is unacceptable to grieve. The baby is unceremoniously disposed of as though it had never existed. The grief may come later and be diagnosed as post-natal depression, or be delayed until the birth of the next baby.

All parents need to know and understand about the death of their baby. If a stillborn baby is damaged in some way, the parents' imagination may be far worse than the reality. If they can see and hold the dead baby and talk to someone who is in a position to answer their questions, they will find it easier to come to terms with the death.

Dr Elizabeth Bryan has found that a photograph of a baby that is stillborn or who dies before it can be taken home can be of tremendous solace to parents and later to a surviving twin. It will also help to separate the two babies in the mother's mind. Even a picture of the final scan can be helpful. Parents also need to know whether their babies were identical or non-identical.

If parents are able to nurse their sick baby in hospital, even if it only has a brief time to live, a great deal of loving and caring can be given during its short life and parents can feel that they did all they could for their baby. This can make it easier to let him go, and if there is a surviving twin the parents can be freed to love the remaining baby. However, before they can do so the parents need some space to grieve on their own. Perhaps the mother could be moved to a smaller side-ward and given extra visiting time to be with her husband and family. The importance of parents sharing their grief cannot be emphasized too much, or each may build a wall around their feelings which can cause lasting damage to their relationship. If there is no period of mourning, the grief may return later under a different guise.

Hospitals can sometimes be in too much of a hurry to dispose of a dead baby and, in the midst of their grief, many parents do not realize that they could have a small ceremony and a proper burial. Parents have said that they have sometimes doubted the reality of the second baby, but a shared service and a tiny grave, or perhaps a rose bush planted in the garden of remembrance can give their memory a focal point.

After the first shock and disbelief, feelings of anger may be uppermost in the parents' minds. Why did the doctors not save him? Why did they not respond to signals from the mother that something was wrong? Endless questions that need patient answers. Sometimes the parents' anger may be turned against the partner or against the surviving twin. What right had he to survive when his twin died? He must have been too greedy, too big, a cuckoo in the nest destroying his brother. The dead twin becomes idealized, perfect, deserving of love, the survivor undeserving, a usurper, the bad baby. If a mother becomes stuck in her anger, then professional help will usually assist her to move on, but the anger is a natural stage in grieving and, if understood and shared, will gradually decrease. A mother who is aware of her feelings towards the surviving baby, but finds them unacceptable, may compensate by over-indulging the child so that he becomes powerful and difficult. She is unable to be firm but finds it progressively harder to control her angry feelings. He becomes the bad child of her imagination.

Once the mother understands that these feelings are normal and will pass and that she is not helping the surviving child by indulging him, she can begin to set limits and refuse to respond to bids for negative attention. Good behaviour is rewarded with praise. Once the child has learned that 'no' means 'no' and has found how he can please his mother, a loving relationship can grow and the child will be freed from a growing belief in his own badness.

Another aspect of grief is a loss of faith in life itself, a loss of confidence that a child can survive or that the parent is able to protect him. This loss of confidence can be seen in children who have lost one parent and who will not let the other parent out of their sight. This same instinct may cause a parent to over-protect the surviving child, particularly after the cot death of one twin. It is known that there is a greater risk to the surviving twin, but this is principally within the first few days, and parents can feel more confident once a month has passed. However, even when the co-twin died at birth and the survivor is a healthy baby, parents may transmit their worries and fears to him.

Surviving twins are sometimes said to be lonely children, but a child who lacks confidence in himself will often find it difficult to make friends. He may also be a child who finds it difficult to cope with the rough and tumble of the playground.

Loving parents can find it difficult to be cross or deny the child what he wants if he is a precious survivor, and this, too, can contribute to difficulties that he may have in making relationships.

For a child to feel really secure, he needs limits and guidelines and parents who have faith that he will be able to deal with life. Even if they feel that he is vulnerable, they can sometimes manage to disguise their feelings and give him a little push into the world. If he feels that his parents believe in him he will surprise them and himself, and all concerned will gain a real sense of confidence in his ability to tackle life on his own.

Sudden death always carries a stronger sense of guilt, whoever it is, at whatever age. The endless self-questioning. Even more so in the case of a cot death, where there simply are no answers to be found, and yet they are continually sought. The parents feel that if they can find answers, then perhaps they can protect the other twin; without answers, how can they help him? And there is the guilt over things left undone that could have been done, of having been tired and perhaps irritable and impatient, with a child irretrievably lost. Of not having picked up the cuddly toy the day before when he dropped it.

If we are given a little time to show we care and to make our peace it is easier to live with ourselves afterwards. That is why it is so important for parents to have the opportunity of nursing a dying child or baby. It is important, too, for the other children in the family to make their farewells.

It can be helpful to have a loving mother figure in the house, such as a grandmother or a sister, to enable the parents to have time to grieve whilst young children and the co-twin baby can continue to feel good and lovable.

'Michael only came to visit, he couldn't stay, but John will stay and be your baby brother,' might be a helpful explanation for a three-year-old who could feel that his bad feelings had hurt the baby, or that he had somehow wished him away.

When twins are identical, parents sometimes feel that by offering the survivor the love that they would have given to his twin – in other words, by giving him twice the love – they are in some way giving what they owe to the dead baby. They are also acknowledging the survivor's loss. There can often be a special relationship between these survivors and their parents. It is possible that even such young children feel some of the guilt of the survivor – 'Why me?' – and try to justify their survival through their own lives.

The identical twin is more than a reminder of the dead twin. The parents know how the baby would have looked, or perhaps behaved, if he had lived. The lost non-identical twin is remembered at every birthday, but would he perhaps have been more successful, more loving, not have spoken to his parents like that? If one of a mixed pair, might he have been more of a companion, someone to share things with, the son, or daughter, they never had? The surviving twin may live constantly under the shadow of the dead one, feeling that he can never be good enough.

Parents who have lost a single baby can sometimes find solace, if they have been allowed sufficient space to grieve for the first, in the birth of their next baby. This baby can never replace the first, but it can often help to heal the wound if the decision to have another child has not been taken too quickly and the child is wanted for himself.

For parents of twins this is impossible. A new baby can never restore his companion to the surviving twin or the dream of being the proud parents of twins. There is also the loss for parents and the surviving twin of that precious enjoyment of each other in the first few months of life, perhaps longer, because of the shadow of the lost baby.

There are now many self-help groups for parents who have lost a baby, and the local Twins Club will put parents who have lost a twin in touch with others who have experienced a similar loss, although going to meetings and seeing parents who have both their twins may be too painful. Talking and sharing with others can be the greatest help in the long term. If the baby dies at birth or soon after, then the talking begins in the hospital, sharing memories with the hospital staff and then continuing at home with family and friends. If it is a cot death, then the doctor and health visitor may be an added source of comfort and reassurance. But parents who have suffered a similar loss may be the ones who have the most to offer.

The lone twin

There is reason to believe that if a twin is lost during pregnancy, the survivor may be aware of his loss, even if only at an unconscious level, and may feel some responsibility.

If the lost twin is sometimes talked about it will not only help the parents, but help the child. The child's feelings and fears can be expressed and parents may be able to reassure him. The example of the seedlings which do not all grow in the window box or garden can be shown not to be the fault of the ones that do, but one of the happenings of nature.

The longer the twins both survive, the greater the shock to the survivor when his co-twin dies. Young twins may show the same separation anxiety when a co-twin has to go into hospital, as a child will show when separated from his mother. The shock of a cot death will affect all the family, but it can affect a twin's basic trust in the world around him. If the parents are overcome with grief then there may be a need for a temporary mother figure, but many parents find that the needs of the survivor help them through this difficult time.

Because a young baby has difficulty in distinguishing himself from the world about him, the 'me' from the 'not me', he may believe that others have the same feelings as himself: 'If I love, I am loved, if I hate, I am hated.' If he then has angry feelings towards the twin with whom he is sharing his mother and the twin dies, he may not only have feelings of guilt, but feelings that he will be punished.

Photographs of both twins together (for the twin that is bereaved at birth, taken in the hospital if possible) will help the survivor to see his twin as someone separate from himself, and if later the death is talked about and he learns to understand that he was in no way responsible, he will be helped to come to terms with the death.

The belief of a child that he has magical abilities is greatest between the ages of three and five, and a twin who is unfortunate enough to lose his partner at this time may feel deeply responsible and invite punishment.

The greatest help that can be given to a child of this age is to give a great deal of love, without letting the child take the control from the parents, and to give no negative attention. In this way the child learns that he is 'good', and that he is not able to be destructive. The temptation can be to give in to a bereaved toddler in order to make up to him for his loss, but this will increase his sense of omnipotence. If parents are finding difficulty in handling the child, they may be advised to seek help from a child guidance clinic.

Talking and sharing is important, too, although it may be painful to the parents. The child's questions can then be answered and his fears brought into the open. Long adult discussions should be avoided. However, in the case of twins, language may not yet be sufficiently developed for much discussion to take place and the talking may come later.

The closer the twin pair, the greater the distress when one twin dies, at whatever age. For the identical twin, there may be a shock that is similar to losing a limb. If twins have been helped to find a sense of personal identity during childhood, with their own individual friends and interests as well as those in common, they will have some support to help them with the trauma of what may seem like the loss of one half of themselves. Nothing can lessen their grief, but it can be made bearable if every small activity is not a constant reminder of the absence of their twin.

After the acute phase of grief is over, a child of school age should return to school, and his friends encouraged to invite him round so that he does not get trapped by his own fears and lack of confidence. Children in middle childhood are not usually frightened by the idea of death and can sometimes appear quite callous.

Twins of all ages always have mixed feelings about each other, however close they may appear to be, and when they lose their twin, older twins may still need to be reassured that bad thoughts cannot hurt people. These worries may surface as nightmares which often bring an older child to a child guidance clinic.

Not only can parents idealize the lost twin, but the lone twin himself may idealize the lost companion of his infancy. He would have protected him, understood him, loved him. This can sometimes make it difficult for him to come to terms with life as it is, particularly if he is over-protected by his parents.

When a loved one dies, anger is sometimes directed towards the dead person – 'Why did they leave me? Why did they go away?' A baby, a bringer of love, is often seen as an unacceptable object of anger, particularly by children, and more so if it has been a 'good' baby. So the family have to direct their anger elsewhere, perhaps towards each other, or perhaps, for a child, towards his friends and teachers at school.

Sometimes a lone twin, or an older brother or sister, becomes stuck with his angry feelings. If he has had to suppress his grief because his parents have been unable to talk about the death or were too overcome with grief themselves, his anger may not surface until later when it can be misunderstood. His feelings of anger against himself may make him push others away from him, feeling that he does not deserve their love, only punishment. Or he may unconsciously behave in such a way as to invite the punishment that he feels he deserves.

Not only does a bereaved child's behaviour sometimes change at school – a normally well-behaved child becoming aggressive, or a normally happy outward-going child becoming withdrawn – but, as in adult grief, he may have great difficulty in concentrating on his schoolwork. Daydreaming, tearfulness, not being able to answer simple questions may all be part of the experience of loss, but should not give cause for concern. However, it is of the utmost importance that teachers are made aware of the situation, otherwise they may misinterpret the signs. Some children become temporary school refusers, fearful of who next may disappear from their world.

Many children become clingy. Giving them the opportunity to talk is the best way to help them to grieve. This, and the security of a routine enables them to work through their feelings.

All those who have lost a loved one know of the experience of constantly seeing the person on every street, but the identical twin may be haunted by his own reflection. Unlike the non-identical twin who, as he grows older, will leave his twin behind him in childhood, the identical twin may look in the mirror and say, 'This is how my brother would have looked if he were here now.'

Twins who have been bereaved as children may unconsciously always be looking for a partner to replace the lost brother or sister. Zazzo tells of a younger brother who lost one of a pair of older twin sisters. His sister was inconsolable and withdrew into her shell, until he willingly substituted himself for her lost twin. Parents who were bereaved of a twin in childhood may seek a twin in one of their own children of the same sex as their twin; even a grandmother may seek the lost twin in a grandchild.

Nothing can really prepare a twin for the loss, through death, of his partner. If the loss is in childhood, before separation has taken place, or in adulthood when a decision to stay together has been reached, then he has lost not only his twin but his twinness, his accepted place in society. There is a similarity to the situation of a widow whose status in her community has been totally dependent upon her husband. The sense, not only of loss, but of being lost, cannot be underestimated, and it may take the twin child or adult some time before he gains sufficient confidence to tackle life on his own.

It is important that parents and children share their grief. If a child feels that he should suppress his grieving because he must protect his parents, or if parents are unable to grieve so that the child may think that grieving is unacceptable, then it is likely to surface again in adolescence or later, when it may be much more damaging. Parents should not be in too much of a hurry to clear out a dead twin's belongings; it may be better to do this gradually and find out which of them has importance for the twin who is on his own.

When a twin is lost in adolescence, feelings from infancy and the work on separation and identity may remain unresolved. Parents should be aware that there may be a need to work through these feelings with professional help, although talking within the family, and with friends, can be a great healer.

A family that has come through a tragedy such as this will find that the bond between them has become closer and that they have strengths of which they were previously unaware.

Perhaps the most surprising fact is the importance both to the parents and the survivor that even if he lost his twin at birth, sometimes even before birth, he is still a twin. His co-twin is an ever present reality.

APPENDIX 1

National Associations

Twins and Multiple Births Association,
41 Fortuna Way,
Aylesby Park,
Grimsby,
South Humberside.
DN37 9SJ

Australian Multiple Births Association (AMBA):
PO Box 105,
Coogee,
New South Wales,
Australia 2034.

The New Zealand Multiple Births Association,
26 Nelson Street,
Greymouth,
New Zealand.

National Organization of Mothers of Twins Clubs Inc (MOTC):
5402 Amberwood Lane,
Rockville,
Maryland 20853,
USA.

Parents of Multiple Births Association of Canada (Incorporated) (POMBA):
283 Seventh Avenue S.,
Lethbridge,
Alberta,
Canada T1J 1H6.

Nederlandse Vereniging van Tweelingen,
Olmenstaat 51,
7101 TG Winterswijk,
Netherlands.

Mothers of Twins Association of South Africa,
112 4th Avenue,
Fairland 2195,
Johannesburg,
Republic of South Africa.

International Society for Twin Studies (ISTS):
The Mendel Institute,
Piazza Galeno, 5,
Rome,
Italy.

TASK	Not hitting twins in the morning			Not hitting twins in the afternoon			Going to bed without a fuss		
Week	**1**	**2**	**3**	**1**	**2**	**3**	**1**	**2**	**3**
MONDAY									
TUESDAY									
WEDNESDAY									
THURSDAY									
FRIDAY									
SATURDAY									
SUNDAY									

Bibliography

Anthony, S. *The Discovery of Death in Childhood and After.* London: Allen Lane, 1971.

Backer, P. *Autonomous Languages.* Doctoral thesis, Instituut Voor Algemene Taalwetenschap, Amsterdam, 1987.

Bascomb, W. *The Yoruba of Southwestern Nigeria.* 1969.

Bernabei, P., Levi, G. *Psychopathologic Problems in Twins During Childhood.* Rome: Acta Genet. Med. Gemellol 25, 1976.

Bouchard, T. J., Heston, L., Lykken, D., Eckert, E., Tellgen, A. *The Minnesota Study of Twins Reared Apart.*

Bowlby, J. *The Study and Reduction of Group Tensions in the Family.* Human Relations 2, 2, 1949.

Bowlby, J. *Attachment and Loss III – Loss, Sadness and Depression.* London: Hogarth Press, 1980.

Bryan, E. M. *The Nature and Nurture of Twins.* London: Baillière Tindall, 1983.

Bryan, E. M. *The Death of a Newborn Twin – How Can Support For Parents Be Improved?* Rome: Acta Genet. Med. Gemellol 35, 1986.

Buckler, J. *The Adolescent Years.* Ware: Castlemead Publications, 1987.

Burlingham, D. *Twins – A Study of Three Pairs of Identical Twins.* New York: International Press, 1952.

Campbell, D. M., Thompson, B., Pritchard, C., Samphier, M. *Does the Use of Oral Contraception Depress DZ Twinning?* Rome: Acta Genet. Med. Gemellol 36, 1987.

Cirillo, S. *The Process of Identity in Twins.* Rome: Acta Genet. Med. Gemellol 25, 1976.

Cohen, D. J., Dibble, E., Grawe, J. M. *Parental Style, Mothers' and Fathers' Perceptions of Their Relations with Twin Children.* Arch. Gen. Psychiatry 34, 1977.

Conway, D., Lytton, H., Pysh, F. *Twin-Singleton Language Differences.* Canadian Journal of Behavioral Science 12, 3, 1980.

Erikson, E. *Childhood and Society*. London: Triad/Paladin, 1977.

Evans-Pritchard, E. E. *Customs and Beliefs Relating to Twins Among the Nilotic Nuer*. Uganda Journal, 1936.

Gedda, L., Borella, S. *Ego Phenomenology in the Human Twin*. Rome: Acta Genet. Med. Gemellol, Twin Research 3, 1981.

Harris, R. *Boanerges*. Cambridge: CUP, 1913.

Hay, D. A., O'Brien, P. J., Johnston, C. J., Prior, M. *The High Incidence of Reading Disability in Twin Boys and Its Implications for Genetic Analyses*. Rome: Acta Genet. Med. Gemellol, Twin Research 3B, 1984.

Hay, D. A., O'Brien, P. J. *The Interaction of Family Attitudes and Cognitive Abilities in the La Trobe Twin Study of Behavioural and Biological Development*. Rome: Acta Genet. Med. Gemellol, Twin Research 3B, 1981.

Koch, H. *Twins and Twin Relations*. Chicago: University of Chicago Press, 1966.

Loehlin, J. C., Nichols, R. C. *Heredity, Environment and Personality – A Study of 850 Sets of Twins*. Austin and London: University of Texas Press, 1976.

Lytton, H. *Do Parents Create, or Respond to, Differences in Twins?* Developmental Psychology 13, 5, 1977.

Matheny, A. P., Wilson, R. S., Dolan, A. B., Krantz, J. Z. *Behavioural Contrasts in Twinships – Stability and Patterns of Differences in Childhood*. Childhood Development 52, 1981.

Matheny, A. P., Dolan, A., Brown, P. *A Twin Study of Personality and Temperament During Middle Childhood*. Journal of Research in Personality 14, 1980.

Mittler, P. *Biological and Social Aspects of Language Development in Twins*. Developmental Medicine and Child Psychology 12, 1970.

Nylander, P. P. S. *The Twinning Incidence in Nigeria*. Rome: Acta Genet. Med. Gemellol 28, 1979.

Riese, M. L. *Behavioural Patterns in Full-Term and Pre-Term Twins*. Rome: Acta Genet. Med. Gemellol 32, 1983.

Sandbank, A. *The Effect of Twins on Family Relationships*. Rome: Acta Genet. Med. Gemellol 36, 1987.

Scheinfeld, A. *Twins and Supertwins*. London: Penguin Books, 1973.

Schneider, K. T. M., Huch, A., Huch, R. *Premature Contractions*

– *Are They Caused by Maternal Standing?* Rome: Acta Genet. Med. Gemellol 34, 1985.

Segal, N. L. *Zygosity Testing – Laboratory and the Investigator's Judgment*. Rome: Acta Genet. Med. Gemellol 33 4C, 1984.

Segal, N. L. *Cooperation, Competition and Altruism Within Twin Sets – A Reappraisal*. Chicago: University of Chicago Press, 1982.

Spillman, J. R. *The Role of Birth Weight in Mother/Twin Relationships*. Unpublished MSc thesis. Cranfield Institute of Technology, 1984.

Webster, F., Elwood, J. M. *A Study of the Influence of Ovulation Stimulants and Oral Contraception on Twin Births in England*. Rome: Acta Genet. Med. Gemellol 34, 1985.

Whowell, K. *Teenage Twins – A Guide for Parents*. The Australian Multiple Birth Association, 1986.

Wilson, R. S., Brown, A. M., Matheny, A. P. *Emergence and Persistence of Behavioural Differences in Twins*. Child Development 42, 1971.

Zazzo, R. *Les Jumeaux – Le Couple et la Personne*. Paris: Presses Universitaires de France, 1960.

Index